Next Step
Victory

Next Step Victory

A 52-WEEK DEVOTIONAL

ANGELA KELLY

For information about this title, contact the publisher:

Angela Kelly
nextstepvictory@gmail.com

ISBNs:
979-8-9901786-0-1 (softcover)
979-8-9901786-1-8 (eBook)

Printed in the United States of America

Cover and Interior design: 1106 Design

I want to thank my amazing husband, Chris, for his consistent, unwavering encouragement and love. He never ceases to amaze me . . .

I want to thank my three kids, Michael, Shauna, and Matthew, for asking me about my progress regarding the book knowing I would need to answer. You are my accountability people. Also, thank you for all the material you gave freely for this book. A huge thank you to Pastor Greg and Susie Williamson for being amazing role models for me over the years.

I'm deeply grateful to Kim, Heather, Lisa, Deana, Beth, and Rhiannon for their unwavering support and encouragement, which has been instrumental in turning my dreams into reality.

Contents

Contents

Introduction

· ·

Today is the perfect day to start—

As you make this journey of finding purpose, investing in yourself, and growing, you will discover you are not alone. As a John Maxwell certified Life Coach, I am dedicated to helping women achieve their goals and best selves so they can thrive in every season of life. Let's face it: life is hard. We need a plan when emotions run high, and the best version of ourselves is on the other side of the trial we are facing. We cannot achieve growth alone. We need to be intentional. So let's journey together with friends, encouraging each other, and with a solid plan in hand to overcome life and make the most of the character building opportunities life is sure to offer us. You got this, we got this. Grab a cup of coffee or tea, a favorite chair, and let's begin.

This book is designed to equip you to grow; offering you thought-provoking, proven tools to ensure that you thrive to the best of your ability in the next 52 weeks, discovering week-by-week action steps to apply tools to maximize personal growth. Whether you are in a book reading group or reading this book with your journal next to you, my hope is for you to experience maximum growth year after year while diving into the thought-provoking topics, discussion in prayer, and verses from the Bible. Ask yourself questions titled "Gage to Grow" that will inspire daily growth in the application.

Commit to the process and allow it to transform you into the best version of yourself, for tomorrow awaits and the best is yet to come. No matter what stage you're at in life or whether you think it's "too late" to live your dreams, this is the year you open the door to a whole new world of possibilities and learn that your new life is right on time. So let's take this step together.

Week 1

Growth Plan

*Setting goals is the first step in turning
the invisible into the visible.*
~ TONY ROBBINS

We all have goals. Maybe your goals are personal or maybe they are related to your professional life. Either way, reaching them requires not only consistency and cultivating good habits but also setting your goals intentionally and learning to see them as already accomplished.

When you reach attainable goals and healthy mile markers, I call that a personal "win." A win is to be celebrated, and each week offers an opportunity to do that. These pauses are important because they are a chance to reflect, make an effort to show up, and continue to improve until you reach your growth target.

This program will teach you to take one day at a time, one decision at a time, and one step at a time. What does that look like for you? Ask yourself: What is my most important goal in my life right now?

Keep in mind that your goals need to be focused and direct, clear and measurable. That makes them actionable. Pause, write your goals down, and share them with someone. Writing down your goals increases the probability you'll take action on them by 42 percent, and goal setting can improve your chances of achieving your personal and long-term business goals by 20 to 25 percent, research shows. A study from the University of Scranton showed that only 8 percent of people fulfill their New Year's resolutions. This shows how important it is to be intentional and to have measurable and attainable goals. What comes to mind right now when you think about the goals you have put on the back burner?

What is something you can do to take a step forward—just one step toward achieving your goals? Now is the best time to grow! Today is a fresh start, a new day to live and thrive.

What are you doing to set yourself up to thrive? Diving into this book is a perfect start, so well done so far.

Ask yourself, how do I spend my downtime? Do I spend time adding value to myself?

If so, how and for how long? How can you shift thirty minutes of downtime to growth time? What would that look like if applied in a week's time?

A little about the author. When I graduated from Portland Christian High School in Oregon I had options to go into the Army, travel to Baja Mexico, or go into YWAM (Youth with a

Mission.) High school was behind me and many options stood before me. I was a nanny at the time, living with Ivan and Sally, taking care of her husband Ivan as he suffered from Alzheimer's. My jobs included cooking, cleaning, tending to him, and also working at the Vista House at the Columbia River George in Oregon. Figuring out my next step was not easy. I chose to enroll into YWAM in Paia, Maui, learning and growing over the course of two and a half months of training and outreach, and I was in India for two and a half more months. I had to step out of my comfort zone to allow myself a growth spurt, and that was one of the best decisions of my life. Growth takes effort and sacrifice. It takes grit and determination. What are you determined to accomplish over the next 52 weeks? What area is most important to you in this season of life that you want to see flourish? Ask yourself, when was the last time I had a growth spurt? What area in my life have I grown quickly in? What was the cost? To grow, what will I need to let go of to grab ahold of new learning tools in this season of my life? List a few . . .

Identify the season you are in. Are you willing to undergo change to enter a new season of growth? What area of growth are you targeting right now? What have you been stuck in for a while? This might be an area that you think about all the time and get frustrated. Thinking about it is actually called rumination, which can lead to depression. We can wither away if we don't make the adjustments to grow. What is one thing you can do to take a step in the direction of growth in this area in your life?

Key thought—growth is key so lazy needs to flee. Stepping out of complacency is a step closer to enjoyment.

We are all changing all the time. One of those changes can come from making a decision today about who we want to be and then taking steps to go forward. Often we do not know all the details, how exactly we will get there, or what it will look like when we arrive, but moving forward is an investment. Choosing to stay as you are is also a choice; grumbling, complaining, and having a negative attitude is the byproduct.

Ask yourself, what is in the way of your growth? What fear or apprehension is keeping you stuck? If failure is playing out in your mind, choose to have no regrets and see any "failures" as lessons learned. To make that mental shift is to take one step closer to discovering how you are wired. Ask yourself, what would this look like if I were to look at this from a different perspective?

Verse:

The plans of the heart belong to man, but the answer of the tongue is from the Lord. All the ways of a man are pure in his own eyes, but the Lord weighs the spirit. Commit your work to the Lord, and your plans will be established. The heart of man plans his way, but the Lord establishes his steps.

~ PROVERBS 16:1–3, 9

Prayer:

Lord, thank you for this day, for this is the day that you made, we will rejoice and be glad in it. Thank you for the opportunity today to move forward. Lord, I commit the area of . . . (fill in the blank) to grow. Thank you ahead of time for creative ideas to help maximize growth mentally, spiritually, physically, and emotionally. Your Word says that apart from you we can do nothing. Lord, guide, direct, and give understanding in the ways to grow in this next season. Thank you for this time as we read your Word and experience all that you have in store for us. Lord, thank you for the plans you have placed in our hearts and minds. Thank you ahead of time as we look forward to flourishing and prospering in all areas of life. Amen.

Gauge to Grow:

1. Take some time to reflect and think about an area in which you wish to grow. Write it down. Be specific. What can you implement this week to help you grow?

2. Envision what would it look like to accomplish that goal so at the end of this week you are able to check off daily growth intentional steps.

3. Set aside time so nothing will be scheduled during your designated time of personal growth.

Set an alarm if possible.

Make sure you also take some time to write down and record three wins that take place this week. It's important to start out each week thinking about areas of growth as you look for opportunities to thrive. This will ensure you show up enthusiastically, knowing you're taking positive steps toward building the next growth opportunity.

This is big . . . Remember to celebrate the decision to grow.

Set up time to celebrate the wins of the week. We move forward one thought, one decision, one step at a time.

What do I mean by Gauge to Grow? These sections are an opportunity to reflect and commit to daily action. Movement encourages forward motion. Taking steps forward daily creates the life you always wanted—your unique life lived fully, the life you were intended live, and one that makes best use of your gifts and talents. Your daily actions need not be perfect but they should be intentional and they should move you forward. So gauge where you are now to get to where you want to be. Make a plan a year from now, formulating both outward goals and inward goals. It starts in our mind. How you think is the actions you live out.

Forging Friendship

Write down and share three wins
that took place last week.

You are the average of the five closest people
you spend the most time with.
~ JIM ROHN

D o you choose your friends wisely? What common attributes do your closest friendships possess? Does anyone come to mind that you want to start a friendship with? Do you need to call a few people to connect and grow in a healthy friendship? Start with small steps and trust the process. If there are people in your life who do not support or encourage you, do you think this is a time to prune and set boundaries? Draining people drain you! It's like they suck the life right out of you.

Ask yourself, who are the people in your friend group? Who are the five closest people to you from your friend group? Should they be? What value do they add to you? What if you were to set a timer when they call to help set healthy boundaries? This could cultivate a sense of awareness of your energy, and when your peace leaves that is when the timer should be set. This will serve you well as you set up healthy boundaries limiting the time with energy-draining people. Have you prayed for your future friendships? This helps to cultivate friendships even before they start. Take a few minutes to pray for future friendships and the friendships in your life now.

"Show me your friends and I'll show you you're future."

-JIM ROHN

When I moved to New York in 2000 from Oregon, that's exactly what I did. I started going on walks every day to start my day. I knew no one and felt myself becoming depressed. I missed my friends and family but decided to find new friends and grow in a new family. I needed to look forward, not behind, and prepare myself for new friendships here in New York. How do you need to show up? With anticipation, excitement, and expectancy. When we show up excited for what is to come, we enter that space with positive possibilities. Anticipate new friendships as you cultivate your heart and remain eager for the next season; this will attract that which you already are.

I've heard it said that "to be a friend you have to be friendly." What are you cultivating to share with others? What positive qualities do you have to offer? We cannot give what we do not have.

Little do we realize the importance of friendship till we go through something difficult. Think about the last time you went through something. Who was there for you? How did that make you feel? Are you able to let close friends in, not just in the good times but in the hard times too? If not, why?

Years ago, while pregnant, I was at church and did not feel right. It started with pain I tried to ignore at first. I was well into my second trimester and finally got up to go the restroom only to discover my nightmare was being lived. I had begun to miscarry in the church bathroom. I was in God's house in a building full of people and yet I felt so completely alone. As I cried out to God, telling Him this was not happening, a friend knocked on the bathroom door asking if she could come in.

In moments like that, we have choices. Do we let someone in? Do we choose to open the door, and if so, how much? To be fully known is to be fully discovered. In our hurt, we desire to be fully known, fully loved, with no judgment. My friend entered, assessed the situation, and we locked eyes as she held me and cried. It was not pretty. I yelled, she held me again, and we cried some more. I was NOT alone. With hurt and disappointment, the depths of our hearts cry out to be comforted. Ask yourself, do I allow comfort in? Do I allow God to come in when He sends someone to help? Or do I shut them out, allowing the pain to be experienced alone? How can you learn to lean on someone close that you trust? What can this opportunity teach us about ourselves in the process of a painful season? Is there someone you have shut out who you should let in? Perhaps forgiveness is needed. There is not a man or woman alive who has not messed up. We might give grace to others, but we need that same grace. Today is a day to start moving in the direction your heart and mind are trying to move you in. What is something you can do today to become the friend you need to be for someone or to let someone be the friend God is trying to send to you?

Verse:

A friend loves at all times, and a brother is born for a time of adversity.

~ PROVERBS 17:17

This verse is a promise. Good friendships are healthy. A trusted friendship is made in difficulty!

Prayer:

Lord, we thank you for this day. We thank you for friendship. We thank you for future friendships we have yet to discover and grow with. Lord, I thank you for placing me right here on purpose, for a purpose, with wonderful friendships in my life. Help me to be inviting and engaging to the people around me as I step out and invest in others. Help me to love and trust in you and the people you know I need in my life. Lord, you know me better than anybody else, my thoughts, fears, and apprehensions. Lord, I give you those thoughts and I ask you to allow me to experience joy in you. Lord, I pray for joy to be shared with others as I care for the people around me. Thank you for this opportunity, this season, and for all you will be doing in the days to come.

Gauge to Grow:

1. Take inventory: who are your closest friends? Write their names down on a piece of paper. How have they shown up for you? How have you shown up for them? Think of three more people to invest in.

2. Take a few minutes to text, call, write, or send an email and share how grateful you are to have them in your life. If, on the other hand, friendships need to be cut or have boundaries established, think of three different ways to implement healthy boundaries.

3. Call and set up a time to connect and be intentional face-to-face. If that's not possible, make a Facetime call. Get creative and reach out. Think about three things about your friends you would like to discover while together. Show up and show interest in the friendship. Leaning into the friendship shows value and appreciation. What we take time to grow and invest in contributes to our purpose and daily joy. Make today a joyful one.

Week 3

Body Book Ends

. . . .

Write down three wins from last week and share.

The same lesson will appear in different forms
until you learn to respond differently.
~ Unknown

What does daily success look like for you?
How would you describe daily success?

What have you set in place for tomorrow so you can succeed today?

Do you set yourself up for success? If not, why? What could benefit from three improved daily choices?

Today we live fully, tomorrow we thrive. What are you doing to make a better tomorrow? Think about four areas for self-care: body, soul, mind, and spirit. Today, let's look at body and learn to listen to it. What is your body saying to you? Are you listening? How are you thriving physically? The body will talk. Is it healthy? Do you need to schedule a yearly medical check-up? Set a plan in motion to have twenty minutes of cardio two to three times a week. Write it in your calendar, or better yet write it down and share it with a friend. Psychologists have found that if you have meaning in what you are doing and enjoy the activity, you are more likely to return to it the following day.

> *"We cannot become what we want by remaining what we are."*
>
> ~ MAX DEPREE

Think of three things you enjoy doing that your body will thank you for in the long run, adding joy to your routine is a must this year. We can be hard on ourselves and have expectations for ourselves that are unrealistic. Think of three things you enjoy doing that your body will thank you for in the long run so that you can start this week. Our bodies go through a lot in any given year. Our hormones fluctuate every month. We have children, miscarriages, perimenopause, menopause, surgeries, and the list goes on and on. I smoked for many years, and quitting was not easy. I gained weight and found myself in a spiral of disappointments. I was not able to show up for others as I could not show up for myself. Setting myself up for success meant quitting smoking (which I eventually did), meal prepping, and working out daily. Set a healthy expectation and be intentional today to achieve it.

Before the next meal comes, the next day is lived, and the next week arrives, have a plan! Tomorrow is coming, are you ready? How have you prepared properly so hunger doesn't have a chance to dictate your daily decisions? Instead, your decisions should dictate daily healthy choices.

What relaxes and rejuvenates you? Taking a bath, listening to your favorite music or comedian once or twice a week? Write it in the calendar. If you have little ones, set aside some time to regroup and recoup. Better you, better wife, better life.

I started intermittent fasting. Most days I don't eat after 4 pm. This was something very new to my world. I needed to research, train my body, and stay consistent. I have discovered I have better gut health and digestion, and have seen an overall improvement in my health in this new season of late 40s changes in hormone levels.

We have a decision to make when we enter a new season. First, identify what is going on and be self-aware. Name it and find resources or someone who might know more, then set aside a time to talk to them and ask questions. Instead of complaining or ignoring the issue, ask yourself what you are doing about it. Is it getting you down? I had to ask myself what I was doing to improve my quality of life. Lately, I have come to recognize that I am going through "The Change," and that has meant yelling at the top of my lungs (at least in my head) and wanting to cry for no particular reason. I discovered I could not trust my emotions on any given day, and dressing in layers seemed to help if I needed to adjust to my new fluctuating internal body temp. My normal was not so normal anymore. It was time to make a change and do something about it. Even if you have you have done something for a long time, if it no longer serves your body well, is it time to implement something different or take something out that no longer helps you in this new season of life? What say you?

Know your goal and take steps intentionally today to achieve it. Perhaps it's to lower your blood pressure or cholesterol; perhaps it's to strengthen your core through strength training; perhaps it's improving by making any number of life changes. This is a great opportunity to set up healthy habits. When your body is healthy, your mind is healthy.

Verse:

Or do you not know that your body is a temple of the Holy Spirit within you, whom you have from God? You are not your own, for you were bought with a price. So glorify God in your body.

~ 1 CORINTHIANS 6:19–20

Prayer:

Lord God, I thank you for gifting me this body. Lord, today I thank you for the way you have formed me and the way you have made me in your image. Lord, I know you have a plan for my life. Help me to be more disciplined with my daily health to serve this body you have given me well. I thank you that you made me for this day and age. Help me to cultivate my new daily healthy habits for life to serve my healthy living, others, and my family. Lord, I need to see myself the way you see me. Help me to be responsible in the way I further my health and prepare for a better tomorrow. Not only will this help me, but will also set a positive example for those around me. Amen.

Gauge to Grow:

1. Schedule a yearly checkup.

2. Coordinate a calendar with a friend three times a week to work out. Or set aside some time for a bath while listening to your favorite music or comedian to lighten your load and laugh.

3. Plan and meal prep one day a week (like Saturday or Sunday). Start the week with three meals prepped. Write out the week's menus. This will bring huge rewards and returns for your health, daily habits, and family finances.

Turn up the music and enjoy. You could even grab a friend or two and make meal prep a social activity. Incorporating joy will release the serotonin needed to drive this healthy habit further.

Well done! You are really making things happen as you discern the right path to take and then make the decision to walk it. This is essential to your daily growth.

Week 4

Soul Eyes to Realize

*The eyes are the window to your soul
and a mirror to your heart.*
~ PAULO COELHO

There are four main dimensions to our being: body (which we covered last week), soul (this week), mind (next week), and spirit (the week after).

Let's talk about our soul. What are you doing today to care for your soul? I can tell you right now that reading this book is a great first step. You have already committed and have accomplished much by showing up daily and being intentional in personal actions steps.

This is to be commended and celebrated. What you do with it will be the next important thing.

Think about other ways you can care for your soul. Psychology says that tools include the following: connecting with others, staying positive, physical activity, helping others, getting proper sleep, eating well, creating joy, and self-care.

What we look at influences our soul. We notice, look twice to see, and stay to ingest. Ask yourself: is what you are paying attention to worth spending your time on? What are you allowing in? Does it add value to you and your core beliefs? Are you quietly engaged in something difficult to stop?

James Allen says, "You will always gravitate to that which you secretly love most."

Be mindful of what you invest your energy into and allow to filter into your soul. Take inventory, know when to walk away, when it profits you to stay, and when to pray. The time to walk away is probably when you start to question if it's right or not; chances are your gut instinct knows instantly when to start walking. What recharges your spirit? A great way to discover this is when you are finished you look forward to doing it again and plan for it. When I take a walk in nature, I allow its beauty to fill my soul. This is a time I also make sure my mind is completely engaged in what I'm doing, which always seems to give me forward momentum. I start writing poems, dreaming big dreams, and planning well for the future. It excites me and therefore is my happy place. Where is your happy place? What ignites your spirit and fuels your thoughts?

Take inventory of what you are thinking about and why. If certain thoughts need to go, here is an exercise that will help. Pick out some rocks, and as you pick them up speak out the words that represents that thought. Find a steam or water or ocean and throw it into a stream or other body of water along with your unwanted thoughts. Speak them out and get rid of them as you throw the rock. If no water is near, draw water on paper in your journal and label the rocks you throw into the water. This act symbolizes that you will no longer carry, think about, or drag along burdensome thoughts with you. If something is not bringing you peace and joy, and not benefiting your way of life, it's time to get rid of the rocks.

For many years, I was unable to forgive myself for something I had allowed to enter my mind and heart, leading me down a road I had no business on. I not only went down that road, I stayed on it for way too long. There was a moment I realized the things I was looking at and dwelling on were not benefiting me and that I no longer recognized myself and the hardened heart I had developed. If you can relate, there is a choice. Your situation does not need to be your destination, just a pit stop. Think about how you are feeling right now. What's around you? Be in the moment of movement toward forward motion. What is on your mind right now?

What thoughts do not serve you well? What thoughts do you need to get rid of? Say it and tell them to go. Did you do it? How do you feel?

Attitude will fuel your soul. Looking at what you could do and not focusing on limitations is life-giving to the soul. What can you do that you have not tried in a situation with limited options? Think outside the box. Get creative. Picture yourself stepping outside your average day into your above-average way. Claim your new next. What does it look like? Draw it and write about it in detail. Let go of the things you cannot control and visualize being free and on the other side, living in victory.

"Keep your face to the sunshine and you cannot see the shadow."

~ HELEN KELLER

Verse:

Because if you confess with your mouth that Jesus is Lord and believe in your heart that God raised him from the dead, you will be saved. For with the heart, one believes and is justified, and with the mouth, one confesses and is saved.

~ ROMANS 10:9–10

And they said, "Believe in the Lord Jesus, and you will be saved, you and your household." Acts 16:31.

Prayer:

I'm going to take a minute now and add that if you have not asked Jesus Christ into your heart, I encourage you to do so. This is pivotal for soul health and your eternal destination. The Bible says that if you confess with your mouth that Jesus Christ is Lord, he is faithful and will come into your heart as your Lord and Savior. This is a game changer for your soul as it allows you to discern things that are right and wrong and to have a living relationship with the one who made you. You can say these words out loud with me:

Lord, I need you. Lord, I know I can't do this on my own. Lord, thank you for sending your Son Jesus Christ to die on the cross. I believe you came, you died on the cross, and rose again to save me from my sins. I now ask you into my heart to be my Lord and Savior. Guide me, direct me, and lead me from this day forward in Jesus' name, amen.

If you have made this decision, it is by far the best decision you'll ever make. Congratulations.

Gauge to Grow:

1. If you asked Jesus into your heart for the first time, the next step is to get a Bible. Start reading the gospels of Matthew, Mark, Luke, and John.

2. Do you go to church? Have you checked one out in your community? Ask around. Get curious. If you haven't done so, check one out today.

3. What do you do weekly for spiritual health? Write down three spiritually healthy investments. Are you growing, sharing, and making a difference? In what way are you fulfilling your purpose?

Mind What Matters

. . . .

Talk or write down three wins
from last week.

Don't be pushed around by the fear in your mind.
Be led by the dreams in your heart.
~ Roy T. Bennett

What do you think about when you first wake up? Do you find your thoughts are made up of negative scenarios? Be mindful of what you think about first and why. Rate yourself on a scale of 1 to 10. How do you wake up? Calm, happy, anxious, sad, excited, full of dread? How can you train your mind to focus on what's healthy and positive every morning? What practice could you implement to allow yourself to excel? Can you wake up five to ten minutes earlier every morning? What could you do to feel more balanced in the morning? Think a few steps ahead in the morning so the morning is ready for YOU.

Our thoughts can set us up to thrive or keep us stuck. Learn to put the filter in place and talk back to your thoughts, discerning if they are actually true. Pause to think about what you are thinking about. Is it positive or negative? Are you allowing fictitious scenarios to play out? Ask yourself a few more questions. Is this even true? Is this helping or hurting me emotionally? Is this benefiting me and others?

The following is a list of checkpoints to determine if your thoughts are beneficial or not. Identify the situation. What are your automatic responses to the situation that come to mind? Do you have a negative or positive mood? What can you do to alter the negative mood into a positive one? What does your face look like? What physical sensations do you experience when faced with challenging or concerning situations? Do you experience any physical symptoms like stomach discomfort, lightheaded, headaches, or muscle tension? What thoughts are you having? Are they true? How will your day look with the thoughts running rampant in your mind? What does your day have to gain with the thoughts continuing? What do you have to gain by losing thoughts that keep you in a negative mindset? How will allowing the space in your mind continue to fuel you forward today?

This is your day, and how you spend it is up to you. Ask yourself, what do you need to do that you have not done yet? Is your body relaxed and fully anticipating the day? Is your mind able to think, retain, and engage in the moment as challenges and opportunities are presented to you? What about your communication with others? Are you approachable? What are you saying when you are silent?

Do your positive thoughts settle you and help you to move forward, reassure you, bring you joy, allow hope to ignite, encourage, comfort while cultivating calm, bring clarity, encourage a solution mindset and opportunities for positive healing? What are some thoughts that you could start telling yourself to move you in a more positive direction?

A negative voice rushes you, pushes you into a mindset that tells you it's too late for you. It causes anxiety, pressures you, exacerbates the situation, scares you, does not make sense, frustrates, causes anxiety, obsesses, makes you unable to sleep, grinds on you over and over, condemns you, makes you feel hopeless and trapped in a dead-end situation, and floods you with all sorts of other negative emotions. Do you replay a scene over and over that ultimately you have no control over? What can you do right now to change the outcome of your day, to call forth a determination that gives you the mindset to find a way? Just because you have not thought of it yet does not mean it is not there for you to discover. Keeping a forward-focused mindset is daily training that creates a sense of possibility, curiosity, and a love of living.

I have a friend who shared with me how the dark of night debilitated her, making her unable to go out after sunset. One day the thought entered her mind that maybe the dark should be afraid of *me*. We laughed as she shared her change of mindset, which was so freeing for her. She had made up her mind to be a prisoner after dark until she faced her fear, called it what it was, and freed her mind. Her new thinking allowing her to stop dwelling on what-ifs and focus instead on being her natural, jovial, "crazy" self. It is so freeing, so liberating, so refreshing, to acknowledge the control our mind has over our reality; what we focus on and allow to consume us can become the world we live in. Get to the source: where did the fear come from? When and what steps can you take today to line up your reality with truth and a liberated mind?

Final thoughts: How do you process? How is your filter? What do you dwell on over and over? Do you replay conversations and wish you could go back and change it?

Ask yourself, what can I learn? Can I be grateful for it and move on? Allowing our mind to wander is dangerous. We need to train our minds with guardrails. If a thought is not beneficial but negative, emotions follow, and time is stolen. Time is a gift; let's learn to use it to cultivate life-giving thoughts daily.

Verse:

Finally, brothers, whatever is true, whatever is honorable, whatever is just, whatever is pure, whatever is lovely, whatever is commendable, if there is any excellence, if there is anything worthy of praise, think about these things.

~ PHILIPPIANS 4:8

Prayer:

Lord, help me to change my thoughts from the moment I wake to the moment I lay my head down. Help me to learn from situations I cannot control. I give my thoughts over to you, including the areas I cannot control and have no business dwelling on. Lord, thank you for being my anchor, my hope, and my foundation. As I filter my thoughts through your leadership and living Word, I commit them to you. Help me to follow you all my days as I train my emotions and thoughts so they do not run away with me and steal my day. Amen.

Gauge to Grow:

1. Let it go! If you are not able to do anything about it, it's time to free up that space in your mind and look forward with life-giving thoughts. What are three positive thoughts that can free you from a fear you might be facing today? Are your thoughts life-giving to you? Write them down daily this week.

2. If the thought is about something in the past, learn what do you need to learn from it, allow yourself to forgive fully, and move on. Forgiveness is freeing and powerful.

3. Determine if it's an off-limit thought. If it's not helping it's hurting. What is the best way not to allow a thought in if it's not beneficial to you? What thoughts could you replace with life-giving thoughts and ambitions?

Week 6

Soaring Spirit

· ·

**Start by writing down and talking about
three wins that took place last week.**

*What you become while waiting is more important
than what you are waiting for.*
~ JOHN ORTBERG JR.

earn to discern the cadence of the day. The definition of
cadence: the beat, time, or measure of rhythmical motion
or activity; to steady the cadence of the drums to a rhythmic
sequence or flow of sounds in language. When we get overwhelmed or out of rhythm, the snowball effect takes place. It can
often jumble the important things in life, making us barely func-
tioning, scattered, and unproductive. This can lead to thoughts
of frustration, irritation, and if left unchecked, depression.

Learning to deal not dread will bring peace to your spirit as you strive to thrive. Cultivating a healthy cadence in order to approach what is bothering you and bring clarity is vital. Perhaps it's a conversation you have been dreading and is stealing your peace and joy. Give yourself two to three minutes to address the facts when writing it down in order to bring clarity to your life.

Ask yourself, what is the objective of this conversation? Do I need to have this conversation or do I need to learn how to let it go? Ask yourself if the conversation will bring you and the other person closer, provide clarity, and possibly heal a heart. Asking these important questions before a conversation can help bring clarity and help identify a good objective. Approaching the conversation with chilled, relaxed body language, and expecting the best possible outcome is so important. A positive mindset is key. Believing the best about people will help you have the right tone and attitude when entering the conversation.

What questions can you ask the other person to see your perspective and get clarity? What questions could you ask to share positively? Approaching with a desire to learn and see things from another's perspective cultivates a healthy curiosity and breaks down walls.

Lastly, ask yourself if you have prayed about it. Be mindful not to read into it as we have a limited perspective and conversation can provide clarity.

Our mind and time spent in an undisciplined way can give way to worst-case scenarios. Pray, plan, and proceed. Sometimes praying and giving it to God is all that is needed. When our spirit is not tended to, we become ineffective and vulnerable to being easily offended. Ask yourself, does this play into my insecurities?

Am I sensitive in this area? If so, why? Do I have a measured response to the situation? Be aware, be on, and be open.

Take on the two-minute-a-day challenge: commit to show up and stay constant for two minutes in a growth activity for your spirit. Check it, correct it. Make it fun and make it something that declutters the cobwebs of the brain; this will bring clarity to your mind. Now go forward with fun, filling your spirit with clarity and truth.

Discover what feeds your spirit. What is it you delight in doing and what brings you joy? Then ask yourself, how can I cultivate more joy in my day? What would my day look like if I dedicated five minutes in three different areas to something that feeds my spirit and causes me joy? Speak it out loud right now. Write it down too! What is it? Say it again with passion and with conviction. This could look like learning how to make a blanket, learning how to play a song on the piano, painting, or planting. Whatever feeds your spirit, make space in your day for it, and let your spirit soar. Allowing joy causes endorphins (the "happy hormones") to be produced. This in turn will produce dopamine, which makes us feel satisfied, excited, and stimulated.

Let's face it, we can't control what is taking place around us, but we can cultivate the space we occupy, recognize when we need clarity, and do something fun that will fill our spirit.

Verse:

For in this hope, we were saved. But hope that is seen is no hope at all. Who hopes for what they already have? But if we hope for what we do not yet have, we wait for it patiently.

~ ROMANS 8:24-25

Prayer:

Lord, thank you for creating me uniquely and wonderfully in your image and by your authority. Help me to live out what you have impressed upon my heart, to grow and flourish. Lord, I desire to thrive and overcome. The world speaks very differently. I want to reflect your Word, your voice, and your truth. Lord, thank you for your living Word that is a lamp to my feet and a light into my path. Help me to embrace your truth daily and all that you have in store for me. I embrace what is to come. I pray that things that do not matter will diminish and what I am made for will be amplified.

Gauge to Grow:

1. Take inventory of something that is not right or could be better in your life. Take a few minutes to write it down. How can you help in this situation? Ask yourself if you even need to respond to this situation. If so, give yourself twenty-four hours to process and see if you still feel the same way and if your response is needed. Sometimes saying nothing is saying something. Stop and think about that for a minuite. Think about the best outcome you want and respond out of that place.

2. What feeds your spirit? What is it you delight to do that brings you joy? How could you cultivate more joy in the day? What would the day look like if five min were dedicated in three different areas to something that feeds the

spirit cultivating joy? Speak it out right now. Say it again with passion and conviction.

3. Write it down. Did you do it? Did you write it down? Did you say it out loud? Great job!

What Is

Start by talking about three wins that took place last week and any prayers that were answered.

Your vision will become clear only when you can look into your own heart. Who looks outside, dreams: who looks inside, awakens.

~ CARL JUNG

*E*valuate how and what you are doing today. On a scale of 1 to 10, how would you rate yourself? What are you doing today that will matter a week from now, a year from now, five years from now, ten years from now, for eternity? Relationally, physically, emotionally, and spiritually, what are you doing that matters and lines up with your core values as to why you are made? What excites you? What brings you joy? If you have not yet made a list of your core values, take some time to do so now. This will help you be intentional about your absolute, nonnegotiables that have meaning to you.

How can I make a small shift to get closer to my desired goal? Here's a practical exercise. When you go to the beach, how do you relax? Snorkel, take a walk on the beach, ride a bike, or go deep-sea fishing? Do you like to take a nap, read a book, talk to people next to you, socialize, Google where to eat, go shopping, listen to music, build a sand castle, or just sit and watch the waves? What does your answer tell you about yourself? We are all wired differently and uniquely. Some of the options for ocean-side activities relax you and some you have absolutely no desire to do, yet all take place at the beach.

Discuss this topic with a small group, trusted friend, or family, and write about it in your journal. This simple exercise can explain your personality and help you see life. It's important to take time to think about why you do what you do. How does it fulfill you?

Think of something that inspires you, fires you up, or encourages you, and do it. If it's a book you want to write "someday," start writing thoughts down today. If it's an idea you have yet to explore, take that next step to find out more information to grow, or call someone to join you in your endeavor. Commit today to take a step closer to your goals.

Maybe you are in search of purpose now that the kids are all in school or have moved out of the house, and you find yourself in a new season. What are you doing to adjust to this new season? Are you excited for it? Instead of wishing for what was, ask yourself what is it that has yet to be fully realized. Respond to your calling! My kids are in high school and college, and seeing them thrive is so gratifying. When we go to the beach, each of us enjoys different activities. All is good, yet all so different. I like to go on a long walk, my husband likes to read or research, the boys fish or boogie board, and my daughter takes a nap. Same place and different goals, but all enjoy unique ways of spending free time.

Verse:

When I was a child, I spoke like a child, I thought like a child, I reasoned like a child. When I became a man or woman, I gave up childish ways. For now, we see in a mirror dimly, but then face to face. Now I know in part; then I shall know fully, even as I have been fully known. So now faith, hope, and love abide, these three; but the greatest of these is love.

~ 1 CORINTHIANS 13:11–13

Prayer:

Lord, help me today as I stop to think about how I am made uniquely with likes and dislikes. Help me be aware of others and their differences. Lord, help me to appreciate differences and enjoy them fully. We know, Lord, that we need you. We call upon you and look forward to what you're going to do today. I acknowledge that I am so different and appreciate the way I am made. We know you will show up. We trust you as we relinquish control, and we ask for discernment about how we can make our lives matter and make a difference. Lord, bring people into my life who I can care for and speak encouragement life-giving truth into. The areas in which I'm growing, I pray for excitement about every day. I pray that others around me will grow as we lift each other daily. Lord, I know I'm not alone. Give me the awareness to know you are right here with me every step of the way. Thank you, Lord, in Jesus' name. Amen.

Gauge to Grow:

1. Stop and take inventory . . . is what I'm doing daily serving my future desired self or am I stuck in a habit that no longer brings me closer to my desired goals?

2. Set time aside every day to cultivate growth in your desired area of calling. What comes naturally to me? What gives me energy and what depletes me?

3. Ask yourself why, why do I do what I do? What emotion describes my why? How does that make you feel?

4. If it is benefiting you, could doing something else add even more value? What do you need to say no to today? What do you need to say yes to? And what can wait for an answer?

Week 8

Maximize Time

. . . .

What are the three wins
from this past week?

*Yesterday's the past, tomorrow's the future, but today
is a gift. That's why it's called the present.*
~ BILL KEANE

We all have twenty-four hours a day, seven days a week.
Take inventory of your time. Where does it go? Why does
it seem as though some days won't end soon enough and other
days we blink and it's over and we're still left with laundry and
a laundry list yet to be dealt with?

What has importance and what is pressing? Let's look at
our time and the things in our life that are of importance and
demand attention versus what just seems urgent but just pulls

our attention from what matters. Allow yourself to pause and ask, is this something that involves me? Can it wait? Should it wait or is it a distraction from the things that make a difference in the long run? Write down the things that matter to you, then be mindful when something appears and appeals to you but has no long-lasting value in your life.

I can get very distracted. While taking a class online a trip idea will pop up on the screen or into my mind and just like that I'm looking up the next place to go as a family. A family vacation is a good thing in and of itself, but letting the thought become a distraction from the objective of learning and keeping on task is not such a good thing. Would saving it until evening when it's time to relax, or at some other time of the day, be better? Probably. That would be a better time to research, dream, and plan the next vacation. Recognize when your most productive time of the day is, and utilize that time to the best of your ability, making the most of your day. How can you maximize your time? Take a look this week and write down what it is you do in your free time. What adjustments would you like to make? How can you be more disciplined with the gift of time? How would making a small shift in your daily time benefit you in the long run? Set aside twenty min a day to . . . instead of . . . for the desired result to be . . .

What other small adjustments of time would better serve you? I love this by John Maxwell:

"I've outgrown yesterday and grown into tomorrow.
I've outgrown old expectations and grown into new expectations.
I've grown in past victories and grown into present victories.

I've outgrown average relationships and grown into improving
relationships.
I've outgrown what was and grown into what could be.
I found growing success, and grown into significance."

That says it all!!!!!

Verse:

*For I want you to know how great a struggle I have for you
and for those at Laodicea [replace this location for where you
are located—author's note] and for all who have not seen
me face to face, that their hearts may be encouraged, being
knit together in love, to reach all the riches of full assurance
of understanding and the knowledge of God's mystery, which
is Christ, in whom are hidden all the treasures of wisdom
and knowledge. I say this so that no one may delude you
with plausible arguments. For though I am absent in body,
yet I am with you in spirit, rejoicing to see your good order
and the firmness of your faith in Christ. Therefore, as you
received Christ Jesus the Lord, so walk in him, rooted and
built up in him and established in the faith, just as you
were taught, abounding in thanksgiving.*

~ COLOSSIANS 2:1–7

Prayer:

Lord, help me to be mindful today of my time and accountable
to the areas I give attention to. And thank you for my faith in

you as it is growing and building up daily. Thank you that no matter what comes my way I can have a long-term vision for how to spend my time and what I should give attention to. Thank you, Lord, for discernment in this area of time. Thank you for the gift of time on this earth that you have given me. It's truly a gift and I treasure it. Amen.

Gauge to Grow:

1. Ask yourself what is important to you. Spend your time in the areas that give you the greatest joy and return on your investment of time and energy.

2. When are you most alert and productive in a day, schedule time appropriately in that period for maximum effective return.

3. Sign up for a class that you are interested in or are curious about and be purposeful with your time investment. That could be a pottery class, a poetry class, or perhaps classes offered at your church, like a small group, parenting classes, or marriage classes. All of it is a chance for intellectual development and relational growth.

John Maxwell says, "Become addicted to purposeful progress not busy-ness."

Week 9

Words of Purpose

Start this week by talking about
three wins you had.

*Half the world is composed of people who have
something to say and can't and the other half who
have nothing to say and keep saying it.*

~ ROBERT FROST

If someone were to describe you, what attributes would they claim you have? What would you change or add? What do you want to be known for? If you were in court, what could they point to in order to prove the authenticity of your words? Would their truth be demonstrated by your actions?

Most people speak about 1,600 words a day. What message are you wanting to communicate?

Think about what you're thinking about. A great practice is to set your alarm for every fifteen minutes, and when the alarm goes off, take inventory of what you are thinking about. Is it beneficial? Is it true? What is another way that we allow our minds and our words to dictate whether we have hope? What is hope—the feelings of expectation and desire for a certain thing to happen?

If you find that you're often losing it or being hard on yourself, regretting the way you handled the situation, there is hope.

Conversation is powerful because words have tremendous power. But you also have the power to return to the point when you blew it and set things right. Take these three action steps.

1. Identify where it is you went wrong. At what point did you feel your peace leave and regret set in?

2. Apologize. Go back and make right for the hurtful words you spoke. Own what took place. Make sure that you keep it focused on how you messed up and don't be passive-aggressive, pointing out what they did as well. Keep it on how you are aware of areas for you to improve. The point is to clear your conscience and communicate where you took it too far.

3. Make it right. Asking for forgiveness allows for healing to take place. Or you can simply ask what you can do to make things right. Actions speak louder than words, so be intentional, go out of your way, and communicate authenticity.

You will be respected more for acknowledging and mending than waiting for it to blow over and moving on. We get the opportunity to pass or try again in a situation. If not handled properly, the opportunity presents itself again until you pass. Humbling yourself and embracing in your mind the power of circling back to make things right are healthy habits worth developing. Let me explain . . .

Maybe you find that you just cannot let go of something. Perhaps it's something you said or did. Whatever it is, circling back in conversation communicates that it is not finished for you and that something in your heart needs to be reconciled. Stating, "I wanted to circle back around to what took place because it's still on my mind" allows them to lean in and hear your perspective and your side of what took place. Growth is the objective, and circling back around, growing and being accountable for your actions and words are powerful. Read the following three scriptures to help you embrace these powerful truths that are so pivotal to your personal growth.

I remember doing this while on vacation. I said some things to my husband Chris in front of our three children and his aunt who was joining us on vacation. Immediately I knew I had overstepped limits when I saw the look on his face. My words had hurt, and my failure to acknowledge the hurtful words spoken meant I had failed to care for my husband the way I knew I should. I never want to go down a road where I create habits of talking harshly or talking down to my husband. I know where that road leads. So, later that day I went to my husband and apologized not only to him but also to the kids and his aunt for what I had said wrong. You see, when we say the wrong thing in public we must apologize also to the people that were around as well. This also I find difficult; however, whenever I think a filter on my mouth is not needed the thought of having to go back and make it right is a good deterrent. Be thorough when apologizing, do it right, and it will become a long-lasting lesson in life's classroom.

Ask yourself, are you learning? When you mess up, how do you make it right? When reading this section, did anything come to mind that you need to make right? If so, when do you plan to make it right? How can you show up, rise up, forgive much, forgive others and yourself? Go to the person you offended, or think you offended, for clarity about how they were affected by your words. Your goal is to attain a good outcome, not further inflame things. This will involve discernment and wisdom.

I will add this too: if you need to apologize to the Lord and clear your conscience then do so.

Verses:

Let no corrupting talk come out of your mouth, but only such as is good for building up, as fits the occasion, that it may give grace to those who hear.
~ EPHESIANS 4:29

Death and life are in the power of the tongue, and those who love it will eat its fruit.
~ PROVERBS 18:21

The heart of the righteous ponders how to answer, but the mouth of the wicked pours out evil things. The light of the eyes

rejoices the heart, and good news refreshes the bones. The ear
that listens to life-giving reproof will dwell among the wise.
~ PROVERBS 15:28, 30–31

Prayer:

Lord, we acknowledge that we need you with the words that come out of our mouth. Lord, thank you for allowing us the opportunity to choose our words wisely, knowing that they can not only lift up but also tear down. Lord, thank you for the life-giving words that you give us every day. Help us to be mindful of the impact of our words. Let us communicate with love and care, building each other up. May our words be pleasing to you. Lord, we thank you for your Word that builds us up daily and allows us to gain perspective. Lord, thank you for all that you're doing in and through our lives and we submit our ways to you, our thoughts to you, and our words to you. May our words be seasoned with love, joy, peace, and grace in Jesus' name. Amen.

Gauge to Grow:

1. Did this topic strike a chord? How so? Explain.

2. What is working? Why? Or why not? Evaluate what have you applied.

3. What else can you think of to do that will help to reach positive results?

4. Think about those results and what it will take to get there.

Week 10

Pause, Ponder, and Evaluate

· ·

Start this week reflecting on three wins
from last week.

Be brave enough to live the life of your dreams
according to your vision and purpose instead of the
expectations and opinions of others. He who has
a why to live for can bear almost any how.
~ Roy T. Bennett

Why is it that we repeat a behavior, expecting a different outcome? When the habit we repeat does not benefit us, we become frustrated and disappointed. What would it look like to shift the behavior so that the desired outcome is attained? The reason we continue our behavior is that a habit is difficult to break once established. But it's when we realize the habit no longer serves us, or perhaps it never did, that action is required to change our mindset so that it lines up with our desired outcome. We no longer think, act, and speak in a way that does not benefit our future selves.

Take a few minutes to evaluate how you are doing. Write down some wins. Big or little, they're wins. As we build on our positive growth, we build momentum to keep going and keep growing every day. You are setting a new tone and becoming a better version of yourself.

Be encouraged and be your authentic self, for there is no one like you. In what areas are you growing? And in what areas are you changing your perspective when a challenging situation occurs? Journal and share with a trusted friend or group.

Great job so far. I hope you are taking time daily to learn about yourself as you go through this book and apply its action steps. Improvement in daily decisions while being intentional is key.

Verse:

And to be renewed in the spirit of your minds, and to put on the new self, created after the likeness of God in true righteousness and holiness. Therefore, having put away falsehood, let each one of you speak the truth with his neighbor, for we are members one of another.

~ EPHESIANS 4:23–25

Prayer:

Thank you for each day that you allow me the opportunity to seek you as I wish to learn and grow. Help me to see areas of my life that I need to let go of and areas of my life that I need to improve in. The areas I have no control of, I give to you. Use this letting-go to refine me. Help me to have a healthy perspective that not only benefits me but those around me. Thank you for my family and my friendships both present and future. I am so grateful for all that you have done and continue to do in my life. Help me to have a grateful attitude and perspective each and every day. Amen.

Gauge and Grow:

1. If you are going through a difficult time, who would you like to be on the other side of it? List three character attributes you would like to see improve within yourself in this season. What are they?

2. Make sure to celebrate the win and reflect on the areas in which you have grown from the time you started this book.

3. Ask yourself, how am I doing on a scale from 1 to 10 right now? What habits do I need to break? What habits do I need to implement? Think of three areas that you would like to be intentional in this week and show up with anticipation of overcoming the obstacle.

Week 11

Gratitude Is Attitude

· ·

**Start this week by reflecting on
three wins from last week.**

*It's your attitude, not your aptitude
that will determine your altitude.*
~ ZIG ZIGLAR

Well done. Take a minute today and process all the progress you are making. Name and jot down areas you are being intentional in and taking initiative about. Celebrate! You are changing your life's course, changing the course of your thoughts, and changing the direction of your life. If it's a generational issue, name it and claim it as not being your destiny. There is much power in self-talk and choosing to continue along a positive path of abundance.

Put it on your calendar or make an appointment to celebrate the season of growth. Have a cup of coffee or tea in your favorite cup in a special place. Be intentional, get out of your routine, savor, and celebrate your accomplishment.

I love to travel. I find I do well when I have a routine; however, planning somewhere new to go and exploring out of my routine is exciting for me. I have a cup that was gifted to me that says: "'travitude' (n): a grumpy mood from lack of traveling." What do you enjoy doing? What evokes enthusiasm in your day, week, month, or year? Take some time and think about it. What should you incorporate to evoke curiosity, adventure, and excitement? Who would you like to join you?

As our kids get older, we have to be financially wise with more than one of them attending college. So we asked what the kids wanted for Christmas, and they said, "road trip." We needed to keep within our budget. The kids said, "for Christmas, we want to be together"; they love road trips. So we listened. I found a cruise leaving Florida the day after Christmas. My husband Chris and I planned, packed, and plotted a scavenger hunt in the house for the kids Christmas morning with ten clues. Each clue had snorkel gear or sunglasses, flip flops, and motion bracelets. Throughout the scavenger hunt, Matthew complained that he did not feel good. He laid down on the floor holding his stomach and he would pop back up to join in for the next clue. He did not want to miss the next clue in our scavenger hunt. I thought, well, how bad could it be? He doesn't want to miss out on the fun so onward we went! After the scavenger hunt, the kids were guessing Florida. My amazing husband Chris had put together a slide show accompanied with the song, "All I Want for Christmas

Is a Real Good Tan" by Kenny Chesney showcasing the cruise we were taking from Florida to the Bahamas. The kids were so excited as they ran to pack and prepare to leave. "We'll be leaving shortly!" I yelled, but to my shock and dismay my youngest son Matthew who had run outside to tend to his chickens before we left was throwing up all over the place. So apparently he was not feeling so hot. What, I yelled out, fifteen hours in the car with this upchucking kid? Ummm no, not having that . . . Chris said, "Don't worry, I have a puke bucket with a lid to take with us." Ummmm, OK, great," I said with hesitancy, "that works." Solution of any kind, I like it. I'll take anything at this point. We need to get out the door. Soon we were all locked and loaded, driving in the car, about midway from New York to Florida and the car light turned on, and the car stopped running while we were at the light to turn to get gas. Nope, not today. The ship is sailing and we need to be on it come tomorrow at 11:30 am with fifteen hours of road to cover. Heck to the NO!

We would take turns pumping gas while the other revved the car so as to not allow it to shut off. We had a new rhythm. We did not stop to avoid the chance of the car turning off and for fear of causing more pukeage (I just made up that word lol). I shared with enthusiasm to the kids riding in the back, "On the ship, it's all you can eat, and we are making memories." Once we parked the car and gazed at the large ship, we all cheered. We made it, the car made it, we made memories, laughed, celebrated, and ate! It was an amazing time, and unanimously all want to go again. We will never forget that trip. Gratitude: how do you find it, get it, and keep it? Celebrate the small stuff because it becomes the important stuff.

"Attitude," by John Maxwell

1. Our attitude determines our approach to life.

2. Our attitude determines our relationship with people.

3. Our attitude is often the only difference between success and failure.

4. Our attitude at the beginning of the task will affect its outcome more than anything else.

5. Our attitude can turn problems into blessings.

6. Our attitude is not automatically good just because we belong to God.

Verse:

Do the will of God from the heart, rendering service with a good will as to the Lord and not to man, knowing that whatever good anyone does, this he will receive back from the Lord.

~ EPHESIANS 6:6–8

Prayer:

Lord, thank you for all you have given me. Help me to have an attitude of gratitude. I know that I have done nothing to earn it. Lord, because of you freely giving, I receive and walk with a saved-by-grace heart. Thank you that I get to make decisions daily that will benefit not only myself but those around me and please you. Lord, everything that I say and do comes out of the overflow of a happy heart. I think you Lord, that my happiness does not depend on circumstances, but it comes from a firm foundation of knowing that I am yours and you are mine. I thank you for seasons of change and disappointments that take place, and the lessons learned in the process. I thank you that my feet are firmly planted on the rock on which I stand. Your Word says all other ground is sinking sand. I thank you that my absolutes do not change as your Word is the same yesterday today and forever.

Gauge and Grow:

1. What are you grateful for today? Make a list of ten–twenty things you are grateful for.

2. Positive reinforcement is powerful. Keep the mind focused on the big picture. Rest, relax, and rejuvenate. In what ways have you seen a successful mindset play out in your life? How is this beneficial?

3. How can gratitude help you to move forward this week with less stress?

"There are things known and things unknown, and in between are the doors of perception."
~ ALDOUS HUXLEY

Week 12

Fear Killer

· ·

Start this week reflecting on
three wins from last week.

*Sometimes fear does not subside
and one must choose to do it afraid.*
~ ELIZABETH ELLIOT

Allowing our fear to become the focus is an automatic dream killer. What if the what-if's we come up with do not help our day? What happens when you feed into a what-if senerio? Observe when we make up a worst-case scenario in our mind; how does that affect emotions? Ask yourself, what evidence do I have this is going to happen to me?

Ask yourself, what are you fearful of? When did it begin? How did it start? Would you like to overcome this fear? What might you do to decrease this fear?

Many kinds of fear affect our well-being or ability to perform well under pressure. We can put most of these fears into four categories: fear of failure, fear of success, fear of rejection, and fear of loss. How do you overcome Fear?

When Chris and I experienced three miscarriages, I had to be mindful of what I was hopeful for and not allow my fears to flourish in my mind and heart. Have you experienced loss, perhaps a loved one you long to hold and talk to just one more time? In the face of fear, you build walls to keep you safe. What do you tell yourself to keep others out or you in? Think about God's help and let it guide you in challenging times. What has He brought you through? How has He made Himself known to you during that time? Have you allowed God in to ask Him to break the spirit of fear that binds you? Fear is like cancer: it will grow if not dealt with.

God has NOT given us grace for the "what-ifs" in life. This means our minds are capable of creating negative scenarios that have not happened, and then respond as if they have. Ask yourself if allowing your worst-case scenarios to be played out over and over lends to helping the situation or heightening the situation. Are you able to think more clearly or are you more confused when fear is leading your emotions? How can you lessen the fear and allow peace to lead you?

Note the fear you dread most. Dread keeps us down while hope allows our countenance to be lifted.

What are you fearful of right now? Speak it out loud. When it comes to mind, do you have a visual picture? Do you know there are only two things that we are born to fear? Those are fear of falling and fear of loud noises. All other fears are learned fears. When we are fearful, it is because of a threat of harm, real or imagined. Whether it be emotional, psychological, or physical fear, it is due to a perceived threat to our well-being. Just about anything has the potential to become a fear if we allow it. When fear is activated inside your brain, the amygdala (the small organ in the middle of your brain) goes to work. It alerts your nervous system, which tells your body's fear response to engage. Cortisol and adrenaline, the stress hormones, are released into your body, and your blood pressure and heart rate become elevated.

Try this exercise. Use opposite words when experiencing apprehension: courage, bravery, daring, powerful, spunk, valor, moral, gallant, stout, strong, heroic, nervy, and gritty. Chances are your blessing is on the other side of that fear when you overcome it.

Verses:

I sought the LORD, and He answered me and delivered me from all my fears. Those who look to Him are radiant, and their faces shall never be ashamed.

~ PSALM 34:4–5

For this reason I remind you to fan into flame the gift of God, which is in you through the laying on of my hands, for God gave us a spirit not of fear but of power and love and self-control.

~ 2 TIMOTHY 1:6–7

There is no fear in love, but perfect love casts out fear.
~ I JOHN 4:18

Prayer:

Lord, help me to walk in faith as I move forward into your peace. I ask you to break the spirit of fear. I am not bound by fear but free to live this life you have planned for me to live, move, and thrive well as I throw off things that will trip me up. Lord, help me to establish my identity fully in you and not in the things I have done. They are not who I am. Help me to live more fully in light of recognizing that I am a child of God willing and able to embrace the next season of my life. For I know you are with me and I align myself with you, whose ways free from gripping fear.

I'm not afraid of dying. I'm afraid not to have lived.
~ WIM HOF

Gauge to Grow:

1. What are you most fearful of? How can you face your fears today?

2. If fear was not a factor, what would you step out and do today?

3. What have you yet to try? What is holding you back? What could you accomplish by taking a large lunge today?

4. What triggers do you experience and how can you lessen the number of those triggers? This will take some time to peel back and reveal.

5. What causes you to have such an unmeasured response? This is an area to look at and ask how could you respond differently moving forward.

Personality Progress

. . . .

Start this week reflecting on three
wins from last week.

*Potential is God's gift to us, and what we
do with it is our gift to God.*
~ MARK BATTERSON

hat type of personality are you? Take some time and
explore a test you would like to take to learn more. What
personality type do you relate with most in DISC, enneagram,
or the Fivefold spiritual gift test better known at APEST test?
There are many more . . . The way you view life is primarily due
to your personality and what happened in your life when you
were a child from the ages of birth to eight. This is considered
your primary formative years. Interestingly, the four Gospels,

Matthew, Mark, Luke, and John, were each written each with a different personality. Match your personality up and see if you can relate to one of the Gospels that appeals to your personality.

The Personalities of the Gospel Writers:
A Gospel for Each Personality

D: Dominating—Assertive—Momentous Mark.

I: Inspiring—Animated—Jubilant John.

S: Steadying—Amiable—Likable Luke.

C: Calculating—Analytical—Methodical Matthew.

You can go online and take a personality test. See what personality type you are. Pause now and look up and take a test as this can further help you to understand how you are uniquely made and wired to receive and process information in daily situations.

I took the DISC test and I am a high I with a side of D. My husband is a high C with a side of S. We tend to marry opposite of ourselves. My husband could not be more opposite to me; however, if we were the same, one of us would not be needed in this marriage. In friendship, be mindful to surround yourself with opposite personalities so as to compliment you personally and professionally. Learning to speak another's language and noticing how they receive information and communicate is key. Study the different personality types. Books that cover this topic include *Everyone Communicates, Few Connect* and *How to Win Friends and Influence People*.

Verse:

For you formed my inward parts; you knitted me together in my mother's womb. I praise you, for I am fearfully and wonderfully made. Wonderful are your works; my soul knows it very well.

~ PSALM 139:13–14

Prayer:

Lord, you know the way I process, think, and move. You know all that I have walked through in every season of my life. You were there for me. Help me to use the creativity you have gifted me to lean into you and your Word that is life-giving to walk out well in my current situation. Thank you for making me unique and so different from anyone else. I am made in your image and I am so grateful that I am fearfully and wonderfully made. Thank you, Lord, for the sixty-six love letters you gave me in the Bible, calling me unto your own. Help me to hear you more clearly today and rest in your plan with a pleasant disposition and trusting the process.

Gauge to Grow:

1. Take DISC test or another personality test. Go online and learn how you are wired to receive information. What did you find out after taking the test? What surprised you? In what way does this help you going forward? A book to check out is Marita Littauer's,

Wired That Way, which is excellent for understanding personality types.

2. When processing a situation, ask yourself if this has more to do with truth or perspective.

3. Ask a friend how they view the situation. Try to learn, grow, and ask questions to enhance your perspective.

Week 14

Power of Prayer

· · · · · · · · · · · · · · · · · · · ·

Start this week reflecting on
three wins from last week.

When stillness is all I hear, loudly I can discern a whisper.
~ ANGELA KELLY

rayer is key. Often, we do not have control over situations
or other people. Frustration occurs when we are at our wits'
end. When stopping to pray, notice how long it takes to recognize God is needed in this situation. Does it take hours, days,
months, or even years to turn to the Lord and ask for a better
way, His way? What would it look like if our automatic response
is to pray to begin with? What would it look like if our last step,
prayer, became our first step? What do we have to lose? If we

have done the same thing for so long and it's not working, would this be something to try to receive a different result? Allowing our heart to be aligned with His heart, the one who made you in His image, involves trust and giving up our right to do things our way. That way, the result we are looking for will be much better. As prayer becomes a regular and authentic part of our lives, we'll experience a profound alignment with God's will. In this way, we were experience remarkable results that go beyond our imagination. This is called a testimony. When something takes place and we recognize it could only have been done by God, that is the power of living out a God-centered life. You realize there are variables and perspectives that are limited and God is not. What would happen if we gave up control and shifted our thoughts and behavior to be more positive? What benefits could you discover in the outcome? Could a grander outcome unfold? Write down a time in your life it turned out better than imagined. What contributed to this better outcome? What perspective do you now have that at the time you did not have? Could this be a lasting testimony you remind yourself of when a difficulty is in your life? What is a testimony? A testimony is discovered when a God-sized goal or God-sized result comes about that you alone in no way, shape, or form could accomplish. Have you ever experienced this or heard someone experience a result that is bigger or better than your imagination or the result you imagined would take place? Explain? Here's what happened to us . . .

When my youngest son Matthew was in second grade, he got a bad concussion that affected his eyesight. He woke up not knowing who his brother was or where he was, and he was so angry. He was unable to attend school for over two months. We continued to pray for him for full healing. The doctor doubled his medication and he was given eyeglasses to see properly. Matthew asked if after Christmas service he could be dedicated. We figured out that what he was asking was to be prayed over at church. So after the Christmas service, we asked for prayer. When we arrived home it was time for medication. He said, "No, God healed me." OK, I thought. He has big faith. I'll ask him again in the morning. We went to bed and the next morning I noticed he wasn't wearing his glasses. When it was time for his medication, again his response was, "No thanks, God healed me." When we took him to see the doctor, sure enough, his eyesight was restored and he was no longer seeing double. This is what is known as a miracle, a healing done by God. Perhaps you are in need of prayer for healing, physical or otherwise, for you or someone you love.

Commit to prayer today. What is on your heart that you want to pray over. Speak it out. What came to mind while reading the above story about Matthew? What are you desiring that only God can do?

Sometimes we do experience healing right away, and others it's times farther down the road or on the other side of eternity. It's not our decision to make; however, the choices we make today aim to allow God to be our testimony, our comfort, and our hope.

If you are not a member of a church, I encourage you to check one out in your area. Online is a great place to start. Make a decision today to be a part of a church of bible believing faith. To have faith in a God bigger than ourselves is to rest in His plan and purpose and not our own.

Verse:

Elijah was a man with a nature like ours, and he prayed fervently that it might not rain, and for three years and six months, it did not rain on the earth. Then he prayed again, and heaven gave rain, and the earth bore its fruit. My brothers, if anyone among you wanders from the truth and someone brings him back, let him know that whoever brings back a sinner from his wandering will save his soul from death and will cover a multitude of sins.

~ James 5:17–20

Prayer:

Lord, I come before you now with a desire to know you like never before. Lord, I thank you for the things that you're doing that I am not aware yet that you were working behind the scenes and working on my behalf to accomplish. I thank you that you are a good God and I thank you that if I don't see the good in it, then I know you are not finished. I thank you that in my life I can turn to you, that I can trust you, and that in you I have hope. I thank you for allowing me this opportunity to grow in my relationship with you and my relationship with others. I ask that I always have an eternal perspective on any situation I face. I give you my worries and concerns, and I rest knowing that you alone are the prince of peace, the same peace that I now hold near and dear to my heart.

Gauge to Grow:

1. Think of three areas in which you feel stuck, trapped, or are longing for a breakthrough in. Commit to the Lord as you focus on the things that you can do, not the things that you can't do.

2. Are you ready to ask God to move in an area that you recognize you have no control over? Release them. Breathe in, drop your shoulders, and open your hands as you picture yourself letting go of an area that is holding you back.

3. Then open your hands and give it to Him. It's not yours to carry anymore. Not your pace and not your burden to carry around something that just holds you down.

Week 15

Up Conversation into Inspiration

. . . .

Start this week reflecting on
three wins from last week.

*Nobody cares how much you know until
they know how much you care.*
~ Theodore Roosevelt

Our culture will improve when we have better conversations. What are you doing to model healthy conversations? What type of conversations do you entertain? What grabs your attention? Does it hold your interest? What do you gravitate to, what appeals to you? What topic of conversation do you begin and engage in that people will remember once you leave?

Ask yourself, are you leaving a lasting positive impression or one that's forgettable? Does your conversation improve, help, and heal others? Our words matter, and being involved in meaningful conversation matters. First, ask yourself what matters to you. Are you agreeing just to be more likable in a conversation? What is your objective in a conversation? Are you here to make a point or a difference? What is the perspective, and then work your points from there. How can you improve others and their daily perspective in life? It starts with a motive, a motion, then a mouth.

A good way to start is to be intentional about compliments. Find something you like about the other person. It's easy to find something wrong with a friend, family member, or coworker. Shift the energy to what you like, admire, or appreciate. Think about three things you can state as a positive. Make it a personal goal to be intentional to add and raise the positive energy of others in the room. Having a critical spirit is something to be noticed and addressed.

Verse:

Do not speak evil against one another, brothers. The one who speaks against a brother or judges his brother, speaks evil against the law and judges the law. But if you judge the law, you are not a doer of the law but a judge.

~ JAMES 4:11

Prayer:

Lord, thank you for this opportunity to manage my mouth, speaking only words that are upright and full of truth, care, and concern. Lord, thank you for the people in my life and the words that make a difference. Lord, help me to be a difference maker as I prepare my heart to see the difference and be the difference in someone else's life today. I want to be seen by you and see you working in the lives of others. Lord, as you lead, help us to lead people to you, to your goodness, and to your truth. Thank you for the opportunity today to notice within myself areas to mind my mouth to speak well and share joy from within with others.

Gauge and Grow:

1. What did your mouth speak that is truth, wholesome, and life-giving today?

2. If something comes to mind that is negative, make a mental shift and speak with careful thought leading your mouth. Give yourself grace. It takes practice to grow in this area, and wanting to do so is the first step.

   Do not dwell on what you cannot do; think about what you can do and make it your intention to go forward and improve. Before you speak next time, think about where the words spoken will take you and ask if that outcome lines up with the best future self you are being intentional to become.

3. It is important to say out loud how you want to show up on the other side of the situation; believe it, and live it. Who can you speak out life-giving words to today?

Week 16

Momentum

. . . .

Start this week reflecting on
three wins from last week.

*Grant me the serenity to accept the things I cannot
change, the courage to change the things I can,
and the wisdom to know the difference.*
~ THE SERENITY PRAYER

There's a difference between efficiency and speed. Fast is good, but faster creates chaos. What speed cultivates longevity and productivity for you? Slow down to take a mental picture in your mind of the last time you were in a meaningful conversation or event at a family or friend gathering. What were the people you spoke with wearing? What valuable conversation took place that you thought was interesting and thought-provoking? What does that communicate to you as you look back to the takeaway from the event? Did you spend more time getting ready, picking out your outfit, or preparing what conversation you would like to have taken place? Did you do any research to find out what others were interested in? What would that look like next time you make it a point to find out three things you did not know before leaving a room? A desire to grow precedes a change in direction. We all have a limited perspective, limited time, and infinite possible outcomes. When we grow and learn from others, we grow ourselves. Experiencing a different point of view by listening, asking questions, and being genuinely interested in others is part of maturity, personal growth, and development. Accept the idea that you might not know everything. Or take it a step further and tell yourself what you think could be wrong. What would it look like if you had the mindset that after an event you would like to grow in perspective and view? What if someone has another view that you might learn from?

In fact, the more I have learned, the more I have found that there is so much I don't know. When we step into another's world, slow down, and cultivate wonder, we discover how they think, feel, and move. We expand our minds. Compassion is stirred and a sense of care naturally arises. Without empathy, we draw conclusions with limited information as we tend to fill in the gaps without any real truth. Too often we let our own assumptions, which are often negative, become truth. Attending to the details of what others are really saying and thinking allows you to discern truth and have positive assumptions rather than negative ones. When we ask questions we are saying, "Your thoughts matter and I want to hear what you have to say." This is where we get the idea that we ought to believe the best in people. People matter, you matter. We ourselves want to be seen and we ought to learn to see others for who they are and think the best about who they desire to become. We are all becoming the person God has designed for us to be. Be that person, believe in others, and become a caring person, which means learning to listen and speak less.

Verse:

And we desire each one of you to show the same earnestness to have the full assurance of hope until the end, so that you may not be sluggish, but imitators of those who through faith and patience inherit the promises.

~ HEBREWS 6:11–12

Prayer:

Lord, thank you for the people in my life, for the friends, and for those who help to bring out my true character as I continually grow. Lord, I see how I need to be more aware to slow down and not sweat the small stuff. People matter to you, our lives matter to you. Help us to care for one another as you care so much for us. I pray for your perspective as we think more and operate more out of your Holy Spirit. Help the calm to be ever-present as I carry the name of Jesus to my workplace, school, and home. Help me to represent you well. In Jesus' name.

Gauge to Grow:

1. Take time this week to connect with a friend and communicate care to them.

2. Find out how they are doing and commit to praying for them for the week.

3. Try thinking the best of someone when something takes place and you don't know what happened. Give them the benefit of the doubt. Practice positive reinforcement and reinforce a positive scenario, allowing yourself to assume the best of intentions.

Week 17

Guard Your Eyes

. . . .

Start this week reflecting on
three wins from last week.

God is too good to be unkind, and he is too wise to be mistaken.
When we cannot trace His hand, we must trust his heart.
~ CHARLES SPURGEON

hat do you see? I encourage you to make today a day of discovery, of what is pure and holy.

Do you know how to bounce the eyes?

What we see and what we set our eyes upon is important to note. Take inventory: what do you find enjoyable to look at? Is it beneficial to your personal growth? Does it speak life into your spirit? Does it give you ideas about how to grow and launch your next steps to discover purpose?

The way we see the world shapes our reality, our experiences, and our perceptions of the world around us.
The eyes have a power to inspire, to ignite a passion within us that we never knew existed.
Seeing with our eyes is not just about what we see, it's about how we see it, with a sense of wonder and curiosity.
~ Author Unknown

Dr. Stephen Covey rightly said, "We see the world not as it is, but as we are—or, as we are conditioned to see it."

Max Planck's insightful observation, "When you change the way you look at things, the things you look at change," suggested that our perception shapes our reality.

David Suzuki said, "The way we see the world, shapes the way we treat it."

Ask yourself how you view past experiences. How has it helped you now? How will it help you in the future? If it's not helping ask yourself, am I hurting still? How can I change my perspective to thrive with a different perspective?

What might a different perspective look like? How has this past perspective benefited you? If it has not helped you, could this hurt or wound heal with a different perspective? Go back to your goal. What is it? Have it before you. How might your vision improve by seeing it from a different perspective of hope? Expectations and worldviews are other ways we filter what we see before us.

In the bible, the word "Behold" is used 1,298 times in the King James version. It is derived from the Greek word "eido," which has the literal translation of "be sure to see." Or, as I like to think of it, Don't miss this. What do you behold? And how often and long do you hold it, see it, or stare at it, allowing it to penetrate into your heart? Think about your cell phone's Facebook feed. What pops up is designed as the result of algorithms processing what you spend time looking. Your phone will actually recognize and cause more of the same images to pop up. What does it say about your interests that certain commercials pop up again and again? You internalize what you see from the sites you frequent. The algorithms are designed to detect both what you frequently watch and the amount of time spent watching and internalizing it. Check out the below post from Facebook.

We value your privacy

We and our partners store and/or access information on a device, such as cookies and process personal data, such as unique identifiers and standard information sent by a device for personalised ads and content, ad and content measurement, and audience insights, as well as to develop and improve products. With your permission we and our partners may use precise geolocation data and identification through device scanning. You may click to consent to our and our partners' processing as described above. Alternatively you may access more detailed information and change your preferences before consenting or to refuse consenting. Please note that some processing of your personal data may not require your consent, but you have a right to object to such processing. Your preferences will apply to this website only. You can change your preferences at any time by returning to this site or visit our privacy policy.

AGREE

MORE OPTIONS

Interesting, right? So each person has a uniquely designed news feed and identified set of interests with the sole purpose being to envelope your time and emotional energy. This could involve flowers, cooking, decorating, traveling, or entertainment.

Take inventory and ask yourself if what you entertain is life-giving. Does it add value to you and others around you? Do you look for reasons and focus on restraints to stay where you are and this "unfair" life? Do you try to use social media as a tool to escape life? Or do you use it to advance others and invest them with a growth mindset? This will help gauge whether your time investment is profitable or a form of escape. Be honest. Remember, part of being the best version of ourselves is being aware of where our time and energy belong and reallocating it if we're getting bad outcomes. For some of us, that may mean putting a time limit on your phone or perhaps setting aside a designated location for a predetermined amount of time, to build healthy parameters around where our time is invested and why. Short amounts a day can add up. An hour a day is not a big deal, but if you tally up a month that can equate to twenty-eight to thirty hours a month. What could you do differently with that extra amount of time? Pay attention to what has your attention. Does it benefit you, and does it help you develop into your personal best future self?

Verse:

My eyes long for your salvation, and for the fulfillment of your righteous promise. Deal with your servant according to your steadfast love. And teach me your statues, I am your servant; give me understanding, that I may know your testimonies!

~ PSALM 119:123–125

Prayer:

Let's pray together. Lord, we recognize that there are many things vying for our attention. We ask for wisdom and discernment regarding electronics and the things that we allow to entertain us. For what we allow into our space and what we rest our eyes on daily determine our heart status. Lord, we need to be sensitive to the things that pull at us and beckon for our attention. Lord, help us to be people of intention so that our lives will be marked and set apart to do your will, not our own. We want to live whole and with enthusiasm. Help us to do so as we commit our time to you today. In Jesus' name, amen.

Gauge to Grow:

1. Log this week how much time you spend on an electronic device.

2. Do you find that time beneficial and rewarding? If so, how? In what way could this be improved?

3. List some things that you find you do not have time for and budget time this week to do them.

Week 18

Relationships: Attraction Is Action

· ·

Start this week reflecting on
three wins from last week.

Don't judge each day by the harvest you reap
but by the seeds that you plant.
~ ROBERT LOUIS STEVENSON

hat we believe we reflect. What we desire we attract. If you find you are drawing in the wrong crowd or unhealthy relationship repeatedly, what is the common denominator? I have heard it said, "what we are we attract," also called "consistent, wrong life choices." When our choices don't line up with our beliefs, we find ourselves on a merry-go-round facing the same disappointments and a delusional belief system. It's time for a change and it's time for an assessment of your core beliefs. This is going to be a week of being intentional and looking at what you believe and why do you believe it. Do your core beliefs bring health and wholeness to your life? Do they provide rewarding, long-lasting benefits? Our core belief is something bigger than ourselves allows accountability and eventually allows us to be at peace and harmony with oneself.

To be intentional in this area is to allow the filter over our thoughts and mouths to exist. We are guilty of hypocrisy if we are not living what we are believing. There is an inner conflict. Guilt is a strong motivator that keeps us in line with our core values. If you have found that you have good core values but have strayed from them, today is a great day to get back in line with what you know to be true. What are you attracting? What is a pattern you notice that needs to be broken? Is there a stronghold that you would like to sever today? What would be the best thing to set your mind on to attract growth and health into action today? Think in terms of physically, mentally, emotionally, and spiritually. How would you put that into your own words? Write down all your thoughts, verbalize them, and don't internalize them.

Verse:

But, as it is written, no eye has seen, nor ear heard, nor the heart of man imagined what God has prepared for those who love him.

~ 1 CORINTHIANS 2:9

I'd like to say something here about this verse. No eye has seen nor ear heard nor heart imagined what God has prepared for you as a reward for a life of love and devotion to Him. For the fullness of life is found in His face, His arms, His truth, His destiny for you. Don't miss the big picture by grinding on a moment of discord. He will make all things new. And what is the reward? Something better than our earthly minds can imagine or comprehend.

What does your best day look like? He has taken that day and magnified it immensely as an unknown experience that will one day be known. Take a deep breath in and then slowly exhale out . . . experience the fullness of joy in loving Him today.

Prayer:

Lord, we thank you for this opportunity to value where we have maybe gone off track and failed to do what is right in our own eyes. Lord, we pray for your perspective, your leadership, and your anointing over our thoughts, our intentions, and our way going forward. Lord, we thank you for your forgiveness when we go our own way. We ask for forgiveness in areas that have not been submitted to you. Lord, we pray for an awareness and that there is a better plan and a better way to go. Thank you for the awareness of being mindful of where our life is headed and how to align with your plan and purpose. Lord, I thank you for your peace that surpasses all understanding and guides our hearts and minds in you. Thank you for allowing that void to be made in our life so that it can only be filled by your presence. Lord, you are the king of kings and lord of lords, and we humble ourselves to experience your grace and goodness. Your Word says, "Apart from me, you can do nothing." So we will call upon your leadership in our life today. In Jesus' name, amen.

Do you know Him? Do you love Him? What does it look like to love Jesus? Ask yourself, do I trust Him? Do I share what He has done in my life with others? Do I rest when I don't know the end of this potentially restless situation? By trusting in the Lord more today, would this truth help sharpen your mindset today as you think about the decisions that need to be made today? Rest in His promises, not the moment that is always changing. In what way can you choose to move in a more positive direction of hope? You do know the end. Do you live in a way that reflects that end?

How could you show up differently with your core belief as your foundation and not wavering news, emotions, or negative surroundings?

Gauge to Grow:

1. By growing your faith, in what ways could you see this as a benefit in your life?

2. How could you implement an action step today in the way you show up attracting growth?

3. How would trusting in the Lord in this area help bring you closer to that change? How would trusting in the Lord in this area help bring you closer to that change?

Laughter Is Good Medicine

. . . .

Start this week reflecting on
three wins from last week.

I am always thankful for laughter,
except when milk comes out my nose.
~ WOODY ALLEN

When Chris asked me to marry him over twenty years ago and move from Oregon to New York, I knew I had found the man I was made for and wanted to spend the rest of my life with. I also knew this meant leaving the life of familiarity, friends, and family for an unknown future. Had I not stepped out of my homeland in Oregon, I would have missed a life with Chris and our now three children, Michael, Shauna, and Matthew.

Instead of dwelling on what was familiar, I focused my attention on the future life I desired and on becoming a person able to fully enjoy and appreciate the journey. I knew it would be hard work. I knew I needed to show up daily knowing I made this choice, and I had to be continually committed to thriving here in NY married to the man I vowed to love and cherish till death do us part. Yes, I have had seasons that were difficult. Yes, there are days I need to dig my heels in and get into a stance of whatever life's difficulties present, and the hits keep coming. I know this is the life I have chosen, and I will be fully engaged and present. I choose to show up and give it my all daily. I look for humor as laughter is often not elevated to the level of importance that it should be. I spend about fifteen to twenty minutes a day finding funny memes, sayings, quotes, or pictures, and just get lost with laughter. What would my life look like if at every difficult situation I started to complain and look back with envy at how wonderful my life was in Oregon? I allow myself to reminisce about how easy, comfortable, and without difficulty it was back in Oregon. See we tend to glamorize the past as "the good old memories" and ignore the reason the past is in the past. Laughter is good medicine. It literally changes our countenance and causes an internal shift. It will help you get your bearings and allow you to not take so seriously the situation that next week, next month, or next year you might not even remember. So be mindful of your thought processes. Don't look back with regret. Instead, look forward with anticipation and preparation.

Verse:

Then our mouth was filled with laughter, and our tongue with shouts of joy; then they said among the nations, "The LORD has done great things for them." The LORD has done great things for us; we are glad.

~ PSALM 126: 2–3

Prayer:

Lord, thank you for bringing us into a new place, a new season, with a joyful attitude about the experience we find ourselves in. Lord, help us not to allow our emotions to become so heavy that they dictate our peace, stealing a moment that was to be enjoyed on this earth. Lord, help us to be drawn to things that lift our countenance, and to share joy with others. We thank you that we get to lean into you and know that what we're going through right now is building character as we await the victories of tomorrow. Help us to find laughter that lingers in our hearts and on our faces. For the joy of the Lord is our strength.

Gauge to Grow:

1. If there was no option to fail, would you take a risk and try? What would you try?

2. When pain is avoided all together, are you learning?

3. What have you experienced that was painful? What did you learn?

4. How could you be learning more?

5. How can you incorporate laughter into your day? Remember, it's a choice.

6. What are some ways you can be joyful regardless of the situation?

Don't judge tomorrow's outcome by today's feelings.

When Anger Fuels Actions

Start this week by reflecting
on three wins from last week.

*The driver on the highway is safe not when he
reads the signs but when he obeys them.*
~ AW TOZER

Have you ever had a situation that just drove you nuts and you lashed out and shared your frustration, only to find yourself with a bigger problem than the original one? I can remember that, early on in our marriage, I was beyond frustrated as my husband was so late from teaching Tae Kwon Do (he's a 7th-degree master—I'm a solid yellow belt if you're wondering). I had baby Michael already in bed, and I was so twisted as dinner had been made and was now cold. I could feel my blood boil as his meal became ice cold. So my obvious next thought was to take all the food I made, throw it into the cupboards, lock the doors, and set the house alarm. I turned off all the lights and hid under the guest bed. Now I will admit this was not my best move, nor am I proud of this highly mature state of mind. I had just amplified it all in my mind. I had no real facts to base it on. My actions would have caused us to argue. In actuality, there might have been no real reason to argue as he could have had a flat tire or run to the paint store or Home Depot, or any number of other reasons why he might be late. But none of those reasons crossed my mind as I allowed MY scenario to play out, making it fact and validating my enraged behavior.

Can you relate?

When he arrived home, I could hear him call out my name, turn the house alarm off, and then leave. See, there are two ways we can respond: to de-escalate a situation or escalate it. After some time, I went into the kitchen, pulled out the food from the cupboards, and found him outside in the garage working. I asked him what happened; we had a good conversation as he explained what took place and I found myself apologizing for my highly inappropriate behavior. I assured him that I would not respond like that again. We cannot handle all situations with five stars but we can learn from our mistakes. See, a couple things happen when anger fuels our actions. We end up doing things we normally wouldn't do had we thought it through. Anger clouds our judgment. The worst version of ourselves appears, which has potential to make the outcome ten times worse.

What are some lessons you have learned when emotions and thoughts run high? How can you encourage sound thoughts that bring calm instead of worse-case scenarios? Thoughts and words can heighten, hurt, or heal. Giving the benefit of the doubt is believing the best and not imagining the worst. When the worst case enters, talk back to it. No proof, no peace completely fueled by fear. It's a no-go zone. Decide what are your no-go zones in your mind. When we place a no-go zone we have predetermined we are not allowing ourselves to think this way. We are choosing to not allow a personal fear to become reality in our mind. We replace new thought patterns with a healthy mindset rewiring our brain. So many health benefits take place as healthy thoughts cultivate healthy living.

Verse:

A gentle tongue is a tree of life, but perverseness in it breaks the spirit.

~ PROVERBS 15:4

We must learn to pray and turn towards the Lord when our thoughts and actions are spiraling out of control.

Prayer:

Lord, thank you for allowing us to be emotional beings. We pray that our emotions will help us, not hinder us, as we navigate toward truth, calm, and a desire for understanding. Help us to be aware of finger-pointing as it reminds us to point our finger back to ourselves. We recognize that we need you. Lord, allow us to think clearly regardless of our emotional state. Thank you for always being with us and giving us clarity as we turn toward you for healthy living, right living, and training. Amen.

Gauge to Grow:

1. Ask yourself, what is the takeaway? What did I learn? Why did I respond this way?

2. Was it a result of a lack of trust, skepticism, anger, and unfounded lies? What was the breaking point that gave way to my emotions and behavior? I think upon this time and laugh now when I respond by hiding his dinner and me. We both laugh. Think of a time you responded with a lapse of sound judgment. What did you learn? Write it down or tell a trusted friend.

3. Think about all the ways we can learn in our past, and if it still has a grip on you make sure you forgive yourself; take the nuggets of truth from that situation and move forward.

What would it look like to think about the result and ask your questions accordingly to line up with the positive result you envision? As you step out and step up, ask yourself a few pivotal questions. Does this need to be shared? What positive outcome would come from this conversation? Is this the right time to share it? If not, when would be a better time to have this conversation? Lastly, health is cultivated from deeper conversations of trust. Has trust been established and will they receive the conversation as a healthy step in the right direction?

Unforgiveness

. . . .

**Start this week by reflecting
on three wins from last week.**

*Unforgiveness is like drinking poison and waiting
on the other person to die. You have to LET IT GO!*
~ TJ Jakes

Forgiveness is essential to thriving, not only emotionally but physically, mentally, and spiritually. I know this is a hot topic as we can tend to associate forgiveness with permitting wrong done to us or letting others off the hook. So let's dive a little deeper into this topic.

Forgive, not because it's deserved but because your soul needs it to be healthy. They are still taking from you daily when unresolved anger and resentment linger in your heart and mind. You continue to give energy, time, and space when unforgiveness gives you a distorted view of life. Mistrust and thoughts of revenge will then in turn own you and make you become the very person you detest.

Stop and think for a minute about what your thoughts would look like if you had more energy. What would they look like if you had the space to move freely in your mind without speaking negatively about a person who has done you wrong? I mean really wrong. It takes energy and effort to be and stay angry. How do you forgive even when what was done deserves taking a step further than they are even asking for?

I had a difficult situation where I dated and almost married a man who physically, mentally, and emotionally abused me. Thankfully, I had close friends and my mom who stepped in and I got help. Much time had gone on, and I had convinced myself that he needed me. No one would understand him like me; I would tell myself how well he treated me and how much he loved me. And I'd only allow myself to think about the good times. The marks on my neck and arms told a different story, though. Thankfully, my mom, being the amazing woman she is, helped me get a restraining order, which helped me to adhere to the court order. When in the situation, I rationalized and downplayed, allowing myself to be a codependent person, no longer noticing myself in the mirror. After some time, I realized I held all men at arm's length. I could not and would not forgive. Interestingly, Johns Hopkins Medical is quoted as saying, "Chronic anger puts you into a fight or flight mode, which results in numerous changes in heart rate, blood pressure, and immune response. Those changes, then, increase the risk of depression, heart disease, and diabetes, among other conditions. Forgiveness, however, calms stress levels, leading to improved health. It correlates our health in our body to our health in our mind and heart." Charles Stone, a researcher, says, "Unforgiveness can keep our bodies and brains in a state of high alertness and leads to unhealthy results. Rumination is when we nurse and rehearse the hurt, which reinforces our negative emotions and burns the event and pain even deeper into our neural pathways; in other words, unforgiveness keeps our brain at a constant high alert altering our neural brain waves."

> *Harassed by the memories of what you can't forgive, your thoughts become malignant toward others, and your whole view of life becomes distorted. Anger begins to rage in you, and it can easily get out of control. Your emotions begin to run wild. You entertain continuing thoughts of revenge.*
> ~ "THE DANGER OF UNFORGIVENESS,"
> The Master's University

How do you know if you have truly forgiven? When you talk or think about that person or situation, you are no longer emotional. Do you have a specific person come to mind who needs to be forgiven? Not because you excuse their behavior but because you can't have their behavior dictate your view of life through a hurt heart.

What if the person you need to forgive is yourself? Blaming yourself can also keep us stuck, inhibiting growth and moving forward feelings of unworthiness. Or maybe you think, if you only know what I have done, you would not be treating me so well. Beating yourself up for a wrong choice gives a false sense of punishment due. What healthy step can you take to put the boxing gloves away and allow goodness and care from yourself and others to be experienced. Self-blaming and doubting are not thriving; we are here to thrive and sometimes we need to be reminded of our worth and value.

Evaluate what you would do differently next time. Ask, what is my takeaway from that situation? What positive spin can I put on it and what's a different perspective I can look at it from? Choose to forgive today and grow.

Verse:

Be kind to one another, tenderhearted, forgiving one another, as God in Christ forgave you.
~ EPHESIANS 4:32

Prayer:

Lord, we recognize that we need you. We know you have forgiven much and therefore you command for us to forgive. Help my heart to forgive and heal. Help me to have a proper perspective going forward, Lord, as you direct my steps and help me to navigate my mind toward your truth, health, and wholeness. Lord, I know I'm not perfect, so help me to give grace to others and myself as I rest in an understanding of your grace.

What is Grace? Undeserved Favor.

Gauge to Grow:

1. What would grace look like if it were applied to your situation?

2. What is the root cause of your hurt and unforgiveness?

3. How could forgiveness benefit you today?

4. Make a list of positive reasons you might find forgiveness profitable for you.

Think it through. In the long run, will unforgiveness help or hinder you from becoming the best version of yourself?

Making a decision to forgive is the first step. In forgiving, we allow healing. Ask yourself what you are learning about yourself in the process of forgiveness.

Boundaries

. . . .

Start this week reflecting on
three wins from last week.

Don't blame the clown for acting like a clown.
Ask yourself why you keep going to the circus.
~ Dan Nielsen

e talked about forgiveness last week. This week let's talk about the B word: boundaries. This is a must when cultivating healthy relationships and ongoing interactions with family and friends. The four area of boundaries are physical, emotional, financial, and time. We can tell when boundaries have been crossed in one or all four areas mentioned. Our peace leaves and we find ourself with irritability, anxiety, frustration, and resentment. So how do we improve for next time? We must seize opportunities to set boundaries. If boundary issues are not addressed, there will be fewer and fewer interactions until there is no next time. Or you find you get together only out of obligation. Be aware of when your peace leaves and why. This will help you understand your relationships better and thereby appreciate them more. How can you communicate that you appreciate the relationships around you more effectively? From their perspective, what questions could you ask to better prepare for the set date and time that have been established and in that way make your get-together more enjoyable from the guest's point of view?

It's important to enjoy and anticipate getting together. Have a clearly defined start time and know when it's time to leave. When establishing healthy boundaries, what is a healthy starting point of time? After deciding a set time, deciding a location all will enjoy is a good place to start. Having enjoyable time and memories to be celebrated for a family get-together to take place is important. Start small and build; if so desired, coffee and dessert is a good place to start building. The more variables you are aware of, and the more you have reasonable expectations, the more of a safe environment you will have to be yourself and have an enjoyable time together. Remember, promoting and cultivating healthy boundaries is part of healing and repairing a relationship. Be honest with yourself and others involved about what you are comfortable with. Some families like to spend hours talking while others are activity-based. Be clear regarding the amount of time allotted for your visit. When we are enjoying the interaction there is more of a likelihood that we will want to do it again and show up to build on the last fun experience shared together.

This is a lifelong lesson that we can learn and relearn. Have you ever noticed that during holidays, weddings, and funerals, the symptoms of a healthy or unhealthy relationship surface? What if clarity in communication could be established before the get-togethers shared with loved ones? Now mind you I'm aware some sad unhealthy situations live among and in family. Do not force and enforce behavior that is not healthy for you to be around.

Having proper expectations is important. What if someone does not possess the capacity to show up properly?

Praying is powerful and keeps your heart right for when they are ready to move forward in healthy relationships. Be authentic and live out of a place of love and care. Love and hope are always there; however, boundaries are vital to allowing wonderful interactions to continue. Especially with abuse and mental illness.

What can you do to ensure the next interaction is a successful one? Define what a successful time spent together looks like. How were you able to have a joyous occasion together? Think about how you envision the evening going. Who do you want to invite that will contribute to the evening? In what way do the people you invite add to the memories and overall experience? After they are invited, are they givers or takers? Are you a giver or taker? How is that decided? Invite just knowing the capacity of the people going so expectations are managed. It's also about managing expectations so that disappointment does not steal your joy. What lesson did you learn last time? How can you create healthy boundaries that allow memories to be made in the future?

Jesus had boundaries:

1. When Nazareth tried to kill him, he never returned.

2. He called out Peter when he had crossed a line.

3. He called out leaders for hypocrisy.

4. He refused to speak to Herod.

Verse:

Guard your heart above all else, for it determines the course of your life.

~ PROVERBS 4:23

Prayer:

Help me to be aware of your peace as I ask for your blessing and favor in hosting and caring for those around me. Help me to be discerning with time, finances, and mental and physical boundaries. I thank you for the friendships and family that I can cultivate relationships with and I pray for each one of them right now as an opportunity to experience joy. Lord, thank you for allowing me to discern what healthy boundaries are and what they look like in my life. Help me to adhere to a peaceful mindset as I move forward and care for the people in my life. Amen.

Gauge to Grow:

1. Ask yourself a few questions after time spent with family and friends. Was it good?

2. Define what good looks like for you. How was it good?

3. When are you looking forward to getting together again? Next week, next month, or next year?

4. What things might you implement to improve for next time?

Do some research. What do they like to eat? What music do they like? Maybe you can set it as background music. What do they like to drink? What's a favorite dessert of theirs? Preparing your heart and finding out what matters to your guests communicates they matter. This is not creating a checklist but rather being intentional about making your time together enjoyable. That effort communicates care.

Week 23

Authenticity

Start this week reflecting on three wins
from last week.

When the whole world is running toward a cliff,
he who is running in the opposite direction
appears to have lost his mind.

~ C.S. LEWIS

Have you ever thought something was great when you were looking at it from the outside only to discover that it wasn't so great up close? People crave authenticity. Words are one thing, and reality can be another. Does someone have a solid marriage? Are their children thriving? In a digital world where flaws can be easily photoshopped out, we can no longer be so sure what's real and what's not. What is true and what's just digital? Character can and must (and will) be tested. Giving up when our feelings get hurt, or when we come to the hard realization that we've been living with a half truth, can leave us with a crushed spirit but hopefully also a contrite heart. Our yes meaning yes and our no meaning no might seem so prehistoric. What would it look like for our word and our bond to be actually our vow, something we could count on, and others could trust?

As I mentioned before, after graduating high school in Corbett, Oregon, I signed up and left for Maui, Hawaii, where I enrolled in Youth with a Mission. I trained for two and a half months and left with a group to Calcutta, India. There, we partnered with Mother Theresa at the mother house, serving and caring for the women in primdawn, working in the leprosy colonies, and serving at the orphanage. Her authenticity spoke volumes to me. As we (our YWAM team) sat and had tea and discussed things of the Lord, we got to see her morning routine, her devotions, and how she enjoyed sitting in her balcony and meditating on the Lord. I remember thinking her simplicity, her authenticity, and her daily routine were all part of a process that had a ripple effect that touched so many lives and generations. I was sitting with greatness that came from serving the lowly and answering a calling through consistent daily obedience. Authenticity has to do with being obedient daily in the small things. Simple obedience made a small Albanian woman into a globally prominent figure who knew her calling, knew her purpose, and knew the value of every person she impacted. Have you ever been around an authentic person?

What would it look like to have more of a consistent routine where the magnitude was just far enough out of your reach, it required faith to get there? See, achieving greatness isn't about you telling others you've arrived, how great you are, or what accomplishments you've made. It's about helping others achieve theirs.

Verse:

For I know the plans I have for you, declares the Lord, plans for welfare and not for evil, to give you a future and a hope.
~ JEREMIAH 29:11

Prayer:

Lord, I thank you for purpose. I thank you for making me uniquely in your image with a desire to help others along the way in this journey of life. I thank you that I don't have to create a unique purpose for myself, inauthentically, but that you have established me in my creativity, mindset, and interests. Help me to live well today in my direction in life. Help me to close doors that need to be closed and open doors that have yet to be open. I trust you in your timing. I trust that you desire the best for me and I ask for grace that I might help others attain the best for themselves.

Gauge to Grow:

1. Establish your Why, then determine your What. What needs to be done today to lend into your Why?

2. Does what you are waking up to every day bring you joy? If not, what could you change or find out more about that might increase your interest and bring you joy?

3. Set time aside today to explore an area you are interested in that excites you.

4. Do you find purpose in what you do, where you go, and where you invest your time? If not, what changes need to be made?

Week 24

Score Card

. . . .

Start this week reflecting on
three wins from last week.

Insecurity wants to keep track of our failures.
Grace doesn't even write them down.

~ BOB GOFF

hat would it look like to have a scorecard? What if you
kept a record of all the good you've done and all the acts
of kindness you've performed, and went back to reflect on it?
What would the scorecard look like if it was a blessings scorecard
that you thought about throughout our day? You could call it
your Blessed and Highly Favored card. Suppose now that if it
wasn't a blessing, it wouldn't be allowed to be given any energy,

any thought, or any emotion connected to it. The exercise is how to frame the day in a positive light.

Like today I opened up a seltzer water and it went all over the counter and floor. I responded with, "Oh good, I now will have a clean counter and floor which I wouldn't have had had this not taken place." I had no frustration or other negative emotions. Floor was clean and the counter sparkled. The other day at school I brought in coffee and tea. It was going to be my fuel for igniting my elementary children into participating in a fun-filled gym class together where I teach. Right as my kids were lined up for me to take them I had noticed my bag had been knocked over, and my amazing life-giving coffee was saturating the counter and floor. I'm seeing a theme. But I did think about grabbing a straw . . . naaaah, just kidding. I cleaned it up rapidly and greeted the kids with the same enthusiasm before my beloved coffee met its demise. Lol, you see it's not that stuff happens, but how does it dictate our emotions on a constant basis? I would self-talk and say goodness, you are negative. Get it together. All is well. It will stay well. This is the story to tell. At the end of the day, what is your overall attitude? Rate yourself from 1 to 10.

And as you wish that others would do to you, you do so to others.

Our Lord says,

If you love those who love you, what benefit is that to you? For even sinners love those who love them. And if you do good to those who do good to you, what benefit is that to you? For even sinners do the same. And if you lend to those from whom you expect to receive, what credit is that to you?

*Even sinners lend to sinners, to get back the same amount.
But love your enemies, and do good, and lend, expecting
nothing in return, and your reward will be great, and you
will be sons of the Most High, for he is kind to the ungrateful
and the evil. Be merciful, even as your Father is merciful.*

~ LUKE 6:31–36

What would it feel like today to take a step forward and look more like God? To be a blessing scorekeeper? To experience the fullness of joy? What would it feel like to allow our thoughts to dwell only on what is pure, righteous, and kind, to be the newsfeed we read in our mind? What does your faith say when you don't speak? What would your resting, refreshed face look like? What are the automatic words that come out of your mouth when difficulties come your way? Fill in the blank . . . happens? What would our dwelling place look like if our scorecard of blessings was refreshing and uplifting?

Just for this week, keep a blessing scorecard, and at the end of the day, evaluate: Was this helpful? Did you need to redirect often?

Verse:

*Love bears all things, believes all things, hopes all things,
endures all things.*

~ I CORINTHIANS 13:7

Prayer:

Thank you for the scorecard of grace. I thank you for the fact that I can give grace to people around me even as I am in much need. Lord, thank you for this healthy perspective as I shift from assuming the worst to assuming the best. God, I thank you that love bears all things, believes all things, and hopes all things. Lord, I thank you for your redeeming grace and power to be able to see clearly those around me in the best possible light. Thank you for this understanding and clarity. In Jesus' name. Amen.

Gauge to Grow:

1. Think of three ways you can incorporate a positive score-card into your daily mindset. Write it out and think about possible positive outcomes. Evaluate and adjust if needed.

2. Reflect if there was a time in your day when you needed to implement this more.

3. Were you tired? Were you hungry? Was there an opportunity to replace a potentially frustrating event? What was the benefit you discovered in applying a positive scorecard mindset?

Implement, starting today and lasting for a week, a no-negative-thought-allowed challenge. Lighten the load with humor. Watch a comedian online or go to a live show. Think of ways to make you laugh, and when you are feeling negative, have a go-to to replace and switch the direction of negative thoughts.

Adjust, learn the lesson, and change the behavior.

Week 25

Change with the Season

. . . .

Start this week reflecting on
three wins from last week.

We can either make ourselves miserable, or we make ourselves strong.
The amount of work is the same.
~ CARLOS CASTANEDA

Seasons come and seasons go. Sometimes we hang onto the last season for fear of change and what that will look like. Certain seasons are a natural time for pruning in order for natural organic health to bud and be beautiful.

I remember when I had three children under the age of three. Michael was three, Shauna was two, and Matthew was a newborn. Whenever nap time shifted for whatever reason, I was always uneasy, not knowing how my day would look. I began to ask myself why I was so nervous. This is healthy, this is good. Hanging on to an old routine often prevents growth. Looking forward and finding yourself in a new season of purpose and daily fulfillment is pivotal. Hanging on too long to a season that is over will stifle you, and overstep and frustration can take place. Know your place, know your time, and know how to be productive in this new season of growth. If you are longing for a past season, ask yourself if that is helpful in this moment of momentum.

What is your next step in this new season? What gives you peace? When peace is gone, ask yourself when you felt it leave. Then return to that moment. Think about creative ways to incorporate healthy routines that work in tandem with the season of life you are in, allowing you and others around you to thrive. The only constant in this world is change. Does it feel like you are caught in a wave washing up on shore? How can you cultivate calm like you're relaxing on the beach instead? Peace is knowing how to place yourself in calm and when to move when it's going wrong. Staying in one place too long can have negative effects.

Verse:

Rather, speaking the truth in love, we are to grow up in every way into him who is the head, into Christ, from whom the whole body, joined and held together by every joint with which it is equipped, when each part is working properly, makes the body grow so that it builds itself up in love.

~ Ephesians 4:15–16

Prayer:

Lord, thank you for the seasons of order, growth, and good health. Help me to walk in rhythm with the time. Thank you for the season that I am in and all that I am. Help me to grow and learn in the season. Thank you that I'm not alone and that as I'm walking through this season, you are right here with me. May the challenges I face today be an opportunity for growth tomorrow. I realize that I can't do this alone, and I thank you that you are right here with me, giving me the support and strength I need daily. Help me to sleep well and wake up refreshed, knowing that each and every day is a new day that you have given me. Help me see it as an opportunity and let go of the areas that I have no business entertaining in my mind. I pray for my thoughts to line up to your Word, and my actions to be the evidence of right thinking. In Jesus' name, amen.

Gauge to Grow:

1. How would you describe the season you are in?

2. What would you call the last season you just walked through?

3. What did you learn from last season?

4. What might you need to let go of this season to grow?

Week 26

Sidetracked and Sideways

· ·

Start this week reflecting on
three wins from last week.

"Take care of your body. It's the only place to live."
~ JIM ROHN.

Have you ever been doing something, walked into another room, and forgot why you were in the room to begin with? Then you return to your original location and remember why. Sometimes we get sidetracked in our minds. We have so many things going through our heads that merely walking into another room without being consciously focused on the reason for entering can leave us perplexed and bewildered. Sometimes it makes us laugh at ourselves. I read a post that said, "If you message me and I read it and don't respond, I'm not ignoring you. I just saw something shiny then I forgot you messaged."

There is so much information in a day, so many things to remember, so many lists of things we need to do, or lists that need to be made. We always have a laundry list of things that need to be done—which usually includes the actual laundry. And those lists are always long.

What is the cause of your frazzled condition? Could it be hormonal? Yes. Overwhelm? Yes, could be. Did you have one too many cups of coffee? Impossible!

So how do you allow space to think clearly? Forming better habits (which takes about twenty-one days) can free up the conscious mind, allowing us to avoid stressing out and giving us the ability to complete tasks more efficiently.

Think of any learned skill. On the first day of a new job, there is so much to learn that it feels overwhelming. Think about the first time you got behind the wheel of a car and began to learn how to drive. There were so many things to think about, and your stress levels rose. But as you continued to learn how to drive, what you constantly had to consciously think about shifted to your subconscious, and you found it easier to drive. Driving then became less and less stressful as you could now drive on "autopilot" due to repetition.

Habits are in the subconscious mind. When we are able to shift our conscious mind to our subconscious, this allows habits to be formed and frees up our conscious mind. This in turn allows us to retain, cultivate, receive, and process more information. So healthy habits incorporated into our daily living allow us to process more information, reduce stress, and grow. This will free up the conscious mind.

Our conscious mind can process around 2,000 bits of information per second, whereas our unconscious mind or our subconscious can process double that amount, around 4,000 bits of information per second, just from our nerve pulses alone. When our conscious mind is overloaded, we feel out of control overwhelmed, and scattered.

It's when we free up our conscious mind that stress levels decrease and we are able to learn new behaviors.

Take inventory of your daily routine and see if shifting some habits might help going forward. Take, for instance, the timing of intermittent fasting and how that discipline can have lasting effects not only on your health but on your mind and clarity. I implemented this over a year ago and have seen a huge shift for the better in my digestion and health. This is not to be done every day of the month, however. Your monthly cycle plays a part in how intermittent fasting can benefit your overall health. Take some time and check out the timing of intermittent fasting and how to heal your caloric floor and clear brain fog as well. This also allows your body to use the nutrients from food to maximize your digestive system to give ample time to process food and clear out excess in the morning for maximum overall health.

Another crucial practice is to think more positive thoughts. Studies show this reduces stress and clears brain activity, allowing you to think more clearly. What about getting enough sleep? The best results show seven to eight hours a night is recommended. What would it look like to set a bedtime alarm, turn off your phone, and place it in a room not located near your bed? This will ensure your brain has time to power down and not stimulate it near bedtime. This includes all electronics, like a TV or laptop in your room. Try placing it in your living room for a month and see if you are able to sleep better and have more clarity with this discipline. Let's start this week.

Another idea to consider is that most of us use one side of our body more than the other. A simple way to equalize the body and and brain is to set a stopwatch and practice an exercise every hour, using the right brain to activate the left side of the body and the right side of the brain to activate the right side of our body. This will help to recalibrate and therefore help your mind to focus more clearly. Being intentional with each side of your body will help balance by using both sides of the brain. An example of the practice might be a simple warm-up of stretching, cross over, scissor kicks, punching for thirty seconds crossing over the body using your left arm, then shifting to punch right, and vice-versa, back and forth. If you can be intentional and implement this daily, every hour on the hour for thirty seconds, your energy levels will increase as blood flow circulates, clearing the mind and cultivating clarity.

Verse:

Submit yourselves therefore to God. Resist the devil, and he will flee from you. Draw near to God, and he will draw near to you. Cleanse your hands, you sinners, and purify your hearts, you double-minded. Be wretched and mourn and weep. Let your laughter be turned to mourning and your joy to gloom. Humble yourselves before the Lord, and he will exalt you. So whoever knows the right thing to do and fails to do it, for him it is sin.

~ JAMES 4:7–17

Prayer:

Lord, thank you for making our minds in such a way that when we feel overwhelmed, you allow peace to resume when we give the overload to you. Help me to be reminded that if I feel overwhelmed, I should take a deep breath, rest, and reset knowing it's a process. Let me remember to take a step back and regroup. Grant me the grace to get back to the basics and trust in your ways. Enjoying my every day is freeing, relaxing, and enjoyable. Help me to be aware if too much is too much. Give me discernment and wisdom, I pray. Amen.

Gauge to Grow:

1. Becoming more focused starts with a set morning routine. Determine what your healthy morning habits will be. What can become habitual for you? How will this benefit you? Track your progress.

2. Set bed time and place all electronics outside the bedroom. Second option: if choosing to leave them in your room, unplug them every time. The more steps and effort, the less likely you will return to a bad behavior.

3. Take action to activate both sides of brain. Set a timer every hour for thirty seconds to help stimulate energy,

activate both sides of the brain, and cultivate clarity of thought. Benefits take intentionality. Try it for a week. Log your results and any improvements.

Week 27

Heal and Inspire

Start this week reflecting on
three wins from last week.

Your health account, your bank account, they're the same thing.
The more you put in, the more you can take out.
~ Jack LaLanne

There are two places you need to go often: the place that heals you and the place that inspires you. Where is your place where you find healing? Where is a place that inspires you? Do you feel rejuvenated after visiting this location? It might be a certain location, or a room in your house, your yard, or a park. What do you do when in this location? Do you read your Bible? Journal? Perhaps you read a good book or listen to a song. Do you enjoy going on a drive in your car and putting on music?

Maybe it's going on a walk with friends in the morning. Or maybe it's drinking coffee or tea with someone you have much in common with, enjoy, and trust. Whatever that looks like for you, make sure you write it on your calendar and make it a point this week to commit to the place that inspires you. Ask yourself what the benefits are from the places you frequent. Remember, there are places that stimulate your system and places that relax it. Remember too that it's finding health that improves mind and body. Breathe in hope and exhale doubt. Literally, feel your body calm down and take in your surroundings. At a flowing stream or the ocean, there are so many health benefits that promote mental health. In a pinch, a salt cave can impart health benefits, including detoxification, improvement in circulation, boosting the immune system, and promoting longevity, healing, and well-being.

Studies have found that negative ions calm and relax nerves. When salt breaks down, it creates a high concentration of negative ions in the room. These negative ions can calm and relax the nerves by normalizing your breathing rate, decreasing your blood pressure, and relieving tension and stress.

So give yourself permission to breathe in slowly and exhale slowly. You can get maximum benefits from this practice by making it a part of your routine. Try this week writing a time in your calendar for Saturday mornings to practice for fifteen to twenty minutes. Or whatever morning works best for you to make this a daily habit. What would it look like to have a relaxing morning with time set aside, intentionally committing to your deep breathing practice for longevity, maximum health, promoting creativity, and decreasing stress?

When driving, I noticed I was clenched and hunched over with a horrible posture. I now use my driving time to sit back in the seat and from my feet up, relax all the muscles all the way to my head. This sense of awareness, with shoulders back and relaxed, will relieve back and neck tension, help correct your posture, and relax clenched muscles.

Do you think relaxed driving would have benefits? Notice how you drive. Are you relaxed? How do you sit? As you drive, cultivate mindfulness by noticing your body's sensations, from head to toe. Are you tense, relaxed, clenched, or lucid? On a scale from 1 to 10, how relaxed are you? How is your body posture? When you get out of the car, how are you showing up? Do you feel a shift? If so, how? What health benefits did you discover?

I can remember when I first started doing this and what my body and mood were like as I visualized from my shoulders down, relaxing as I drank my coffee and watched the sunset. I'd roll down the car window, listen to the birds, and take in all the beauty of the day. Every day the sun rises and sets. You can also do this while observing the sunrise and sunset. Take personal inventory of your body's muscles and train to relax, which will bring peace and calm to your heart.

Verse:

Whoever is slow to anger has great understanding, but he who has a hasty temper exalts folly. A tranquil heart gives life to the flesh, but envy makes the bones rot.

– PROVERBS 14:29–30

Gauge to Grow:

1. Where do you go to relax? How do you feel after? What health benefits are you receiving?

2. How often do you intentionally cultivate the two places mentioned above that heal and inspire?

3. What would it look like this week to incorporate a time and location set in place for you to visit?

Week 28

Build a Bridge

. . . .

Start this week reflecting on three wins
from last week.

*I've learned that people will forget what you said,
people will forget what you did, but people will
never forget how you made them feel.*
~ MAYA ANGELOU

hen I think of a healthy marriage, relationships, family, career, and thriving children, achieving such things is easier said than done. Are you with me? Let's be real: we entered this journey wanting growth in many if not all areas of life. At a minimum, that means a healthy mind, body, and relationships. They would all be great if it weren't for the other person—right?

If we are honest, marriage is tough; we can be in the same house and feel miles apart. How do we bridge the gap? How do we begin to build that bridge?

What does that bridge-building look like for you? I have found some go-to statements that give me time to think clearly and allow the other person I am speaking with to experience the power of words spoken in love and in the right time and space. Often, we speak out of turn, too much, not enough, or we shut down completely. When in the heat of the moment, emotions get inflamed, out of proportion, and we lack information to properly respond. Has this ever happened to you? So, what to do? We fill in the gap with what we think happened and make that assumption our reality. After painting a picture in our mind, we respond on the basis of our assumptions. How many times do we say, "Well, I assumed . . . ?" It is human nature to judge ourselves by our intentions and others by their actions. How do we give the benefit of the doubt, allowing our curiosity to dig further and good character to speak volumes? When clarity is given then gaps are filled. How can you fill the gaps in a more positive way?

So what, then? We should learn to ask questions to clarify and develop the ability to calmly proceed forward in truth and discernment. We can find ourselves feeling pressured to answer quickly and with not enough to go on. Then we assume we have all the variables and cause the situation to not go well.

Some ideas for responding well are as follows. Feel free to tweak them to make them your own going forward. I say, "Really, that's a lot. Can I think about that and get back to you?" Or, "That's something I'd like to do some research on . . . Can I get back to you another time to continue this conversation?" Or, "Wow, sounds like you are upset. Can I pray about this? How can I best pray for you in this situation?" Another one . . . "I need to regroup and circle back around with an answer."

If the conversation is an interaction between parent and child, allow time for the child to apologize. Often after a disagreement, we think a one-and-done conversation is the answer, and it very well might be, though not always. If there is not an allotted time for a relationship to mend and heal, you can continue the relationship with an unfinished conversation and no closure yet. If you continue to let things go on unresolved, however, the relationship may become broken, and then other people and things will have the opportunity to come in to fill that void. A wedge can build between the two of you.

Ask yourself after the conversation if more should be said. Ask if the child has other thoughts to share and be ready to listen. Have an approachable attitude. Remember, you're working with building blocks. Having a model of a healthy dialogue is priceless. This is a great opportunity to hear each other well and become closer in your relationship. Be mindful of the value of the relationship and how it might be affected by an ongoing conversation. Your engagement with the other person is an opportunity to go deeper and grow closer. I'm only speaking out of my own experience.

When it comes to children, I have found each child is different. Activities like working out together, making a meal, or driving to a game, are good opportunities for conversation depending on the child. How you express yourself asking questions during times of relaxation communicates volumes. Put the electronics down and have a place to put them while eating. What do your actions say about what you value?

Ask yourself, what is the goal of your conversation with the child? Think about what you were like at that age. What were you doing? Expand your mind standing in their place with a different point of view. We could all learn something when we are on the offensive instead of the defensive. All conversations build on each other. Every interaction is positive or negative, and we adjust our boundaries upon each interaction. Lastly, assess the moment, are you or another person hungry, tired, around others, or need to gather your thoughts to understand the depth of the conversation with clarity. Write down helpful questions to ask that would help the conversation progress in a healthy way.

Verse:

A greedy man stirs up strife, but the one who trusts in the Lord will be enriched. Whoever trusts in his own mind is a fool, but he who walks in wisdom will be delivered.

~ PROVERBS 28:25–26

Prayer:

Lord, we look to you for every bridge we build to be on solid ground. We desire to build on truth. Your truth. Build our lives on truth. May our life be set on a foundation of love and light. Lord, we pray for deeper compassion and better communication. Help us to notice when someone in our family is in need and a conversation is required for a loving relationship to transpire.

Lord, please grant us the grace to go out of our way and help our loved ones see you. We need you, Lord. Today we need your tender hand of mercy and grace. Amen.

Gauge to Grow

DEFUSE:

1. Determine if it's the right time to talk.

2. Execute: Have a "go to" sentence or statement ready, like, "What do you mean?" or "Can you elaborate?"

3. Find out the underlying issue. What is not being said? What can be done differently next time?

4. Unexpected conversation is to be expected. Anticipate that people in your life think differently, and cultivate a desire to learn from each other.

5. Be self-aware: Are you able to have this conversation right now? When would be a better time? "I would like to talk to you later, so when is a good time for you?" you might say. Or, "Let's circle back around and talk more after." Then you can shower, eat, or do something else as you think about it a bit.

6. Elevate your relationship: nothing matters more than the other person. When others feel valued and cared for, it communicates care and love. This will depend on the relationship as you build it daily.

Week 29

Comfort Space Growth Place

. . . .

Start this week reflecting on
three wins from last week.

Not all who wander are lost.
~ J.R.R. Tolkien

When I travel, it's an adventure. What do you find is an adventure? What excites you? What do you enjoy? When I was out of high school and discovering really what I wanted to do with so many options at my finger tips, I was taking care of a man who was ill with Alzheimer's. I would cook and clean for him while attending Corbett High School in Oregon. Halfway through the year, I discovered that I was going in the wrong direction and was given the opportunity to switch schools to Portland Christian High School in Portland, Oregon, my senior year. This is when I realized what I wanted and the steps needed to get me there were not working, and this new school, new friends, and new perspective were just what was needed to start anew. I started actually going to my classes and making good grades. I found a sense of purpose and a reason to do well and actually care about my education.

After graduating in '95 I was given the opportunity to go with a friend to Maui, Hawaii, in Paia with Youth with a Mission for two and a half months' training and two and a half months' outreach. Again, this allied with my new sense of direction, of finding purpose, and learning to be other-minded and not so consumed with self. While on outreach in India, as I mentioned above, I had the privilege of meeting Mother Teresa. I would like to say more about that experience here. She was kind, wise, and loving. Our YWAM team partnered with The Mother House in Calcutta and worked with orphans, a leper colony, and Prem Dan (a place Mother Teresa started for the terminally ill in India). Those were some of the hardest days of my life and the most eye-opening. It was service to others, and in this I found fulfillment. What are some ways that you find yourself desiring to gain a new perspective? What would it take to expand your horizons even more? Would serving be an option for you? If so, where? How can you serve? In this you will find another opportunity for growth. Growth takes stepping outside of your comfort space and expanding into your growth place. Being stuck in the same mindset is not growing. Think about a way you have grown these past few months. What did that look like? What did you learn? What steps did you take? How did that make you feel? How can you take a step to grow this week or this month? What direction are you going in? Does serving help in growing yourself and others? If so how?

Verse:

Every good gift and every perfect gift is from above, coming down from the Father of lights, with whom there is no variation or shadow due to change. Of his own will, he brought us forth by the word of truth, that we should be a kind of first fruits of his creatures.

~ JAMES 1:17–18

Prayer:

Lord, thank you for the opportunity to look beyond my own life and look into the lives of others. Lord, with a grateful heart I thank you for the opportunity to serve. Lord, as I begin looking for different areas in which to serve, help me to be intentional with my time and the people I've yet to pour into. I pray that those around me will be encouraged as I am encouraged in you.

Gauge to Grow:

1. Where can you serve in your area?

2. Who do you know who might want to do this with you?

3. List three places you would like to call and set up a time to meet and check out the organization.

Week 30

Pareto Principle

· ·

Start this week reflecting on
three wins from last week.

*Tell me what you pay attention to
and I will tell you who you are.*
~ Jose' Ortega y Gasset

Let's talk about the Pareto Principle. In a nutshell, if you are
to do the top 20 percent of your to-do list, that will yield
an 80 percent return on your effort. In simple terms, it means
the 80/20 Rule includes the idea that about 80 percent of your
outcomes come from 20 percent of your effort. Are you focused
on what gives the most return? What is your attention on and
is it making a difference, or are you fretting and stressed about
things you have no control over? Look at what matters most in

your life right now. Are you devoting the most productive time of your day to increase the maximum impact?

Ask yourself the following questions:

What is required of me? What must I do first today?
What gives me the greatest return? What should I do next?
What do I find most rewarding? What do I love to do?
What brings a smile to my face? What is most on my mind to share with others?

When we show up eager to accomplish the task at hand, a joyful attitude translates into accomplishment. The task is no longer just a task; it's an enjoyable activity that brings accomplishment. At home, what is a character trait that you are working on to improve? If it's patience, then an opportunity will present itself for patience to be applied to allow for growth. What you are focused on will grow. What are you doing to make it grow? Or are you in the way? Think of the 80/20 Rule. How does that apply to your life?

When we were talking about having kids, and before Chris I did all that I could not to have them, so this was new territory. My husband came from a family of ten so when he suggested we have a large family, I knew I needed to be ready (and I was not). So, we all need to decide whether we are going to embrace or deflect what is new. Ask yourself how you handle the next step, and then you will either embrace it or deflect it, giving excuses, or we can rationalize. So, in my own case, I began to prepare. I began going on walks and praying for the future children I would have and their future spouses some day far, far down the road, who they would meet and marry, and their future children. It all starts in the mind. I was sewing seeds of future hope and promise. I then started reading books and listening to women who raised their children in a way that lined up with the outcome I wanted. I read *Growing Kids God's Way* by the Ezzos. I would watch healthy interactions between mother and child as well as unhealthy ones that I knew I did not want as a way to learn and grow. A big part of being teachable and transparent is asking questions and talking things over with your spouse. After I'd had three children (and three miscarriages), I had a trusted older friend over once a month who had three children, and I would make her lunch and ask her about the areas I should work on and what she would do. I would ask her advice on how I should do things differently to reach the goal of a healthy household. I trusted her, and I appreciated her time and investment in my life. My family was all the way in Oregon and I was in need of guidance. After she left I would apply her advice. In many regards, she was my life coach.

Since I'd never had children before, I realized I had one chance to build a healthy family. I know we do not get do-overs. No mulligans. Being teachable was key for me. I couldn't just pretend like I had it all together. The objective is to thrive in my marriage with my husband. Remembering your why keeps you grounded. Why am I here, what are the reasons I refuse to change, what areas have I changed, and what is the result in my daily life?

Have I drifted? If so, in what areas? Have I compromised? Where will this road take me?

How do I make each day count? Where daily do I exert effort that counts?

Verse:

I perceived that there is nothing better for them than to be joyful and to do good as long as they live; also that everyone should eat and drink and take pleasure in all his toil—this is God's gift to man. I perceived that whatever God does endures forever; nothing can be added to it, nor anything taken from it. God has done it, so that people fear before him.

~ ECCLESIASTES 3:12–14

Prayer:

Lord, help me today to devote my attention to the things that matter, and for the things that don't, I pray that I can leave them on the wayside as my attention cannot be divided. Life is precious and the purpose that you have me here for in this time and in this season is called into existence and ordained by you. Help me to be intentional with the things that I pay attention to and focus on as I use my gifts and talents to pour into others. I pray for your leadership and direction for lasting effects in my life and those around me. I asked this in Jesus' Name. Amen.

Gauge to Grow:

1. Identify where you are giving 20 percent of your best.

2. What matters most to you right now in life?

3. How are you preparing for the next step being intentional, transparent, and teachable? If you have not let someone in, is that something you would like to do? What step might you take to begin?

Week 31

Mindful Meditation

Start this week reflecting on
three wins from last week.

*We cannot become what we need to be
by remaining what we are.*
~ Max DePree

Keep a tally of what you are allowing to play over and over in your mind. To meditate or to pause an experience, Selah. The Bible says in Psalms to pause and ponder. What are you taking into your mind and allowing to be cultivated into your heart? Is it true, is it accurate, is it helpful, is it life-giving? Five years from now, will it matter? A great book to help cultivate your mind and thoughts is *As a Man Thinketh* by James Allen.

I can just hear you saying, "You don't know my story." I can see you silently hold back the tears of disappointment at the fact that you are not where you thought you would be right now in life. Whether you have seen this coming for a while or you are surprised by something taking place in your your life, this book is a great way to take hold of your thoughts, actions, and life as you prepare for the next season of life. This book is designed for you to read every year and apply more action steps in your ever-evolving world of influence.

This life is not set up to be rainbows and unicorns. That's why we need to put on our big girl pants, make choices, and speak life-giving words of hope to others. Perhaps you have not experienced the breakthrough yet. I do mean *yet*. But it's coming. My question is, are you the person on the other side of the season of suck who will one day appreciate this season and cultivate character while learning what you are needing to learn to grow and receive well what is to come? Keep in mind that life is 30 percent what happens to you and 70 percent what it does IN you. You decide today. What is it going to be? Go forward in growth or continue to have a victim mindset. Have you reached your end and are you ready for something new? It's your life, so draw some boundaries. Be awake and committed to your purpose. What has momentum to stir your heart to show up daily? What excites you? What is your truth? What are your three words of truth you can stand on? Do you live truth with action? Ask yourself what would benefit your ongoing growth today.

Verse:

Therefore, since we are surrounded by so great a cloud of witnesses, let us also lay aside every weight, and sin which clings so closely, and let us run with endurance the race that is set before us, looking to Jesus, the founder and perfecter of our faith, who for the joy that was set before him endured the cross, despising the shame, and is seated at the right hand of the throne of God.

~ HEBREWS 12:1-2

Prayer:

Lord, we come before you today with hope in the things to come. As we think, dwell, and move, help us to move in the direction that fulfills the reason we were made. Lord, I trust in you with the next step. As doors open, help me to look not only for the door but the windows and cracks in the doors that provide an opportunity for me. Thank you, Lord, for my joy is in you. Help me to be strengthened and not overwhelmed, to be energized with anticipation. Lord, I need to dig deeper into my calling and trust you as I move forward today. Amen.

Gauge to Grow:

1. Let go of three things that do not benefit you. What are they?

2. Name them and release them. Often we think we have control, but that's too often illusory. Releasing the grip a

false sense of control has on our life allows us the freedom to live released from worry and draining thoughts that literally leave us unnecessarily tired, feeling lost, or sleep deprived, and alters our appetite and steals our peace. Well, today is the day! It's time to get it back.

3. What is standing in my way that hurts my heart when I think about it? Give it to the Lord today. Determine what you do have control over, then choose to live fully and without a divided heart or mind.

Week 32

Brighter and Better

. . . .

Start this week reflecting on
three wins from last week.

Try not to become a man of success,
but rather try to become a man of value.
~ ALBERT EINSTEIN

What is the first thing you tell yourself when you wake up each day? I asked someone this question and her reply every morning was, "Oh NO—it's another day." Or is it, "O Lord help me . . . ?" Be honest. What do you think about first thing in the morning? Be mindful of your last thoughts of the evening. Do you allow space to think about and prepare for the next day? What is your self-talk like? Do you give yourself time to wind down reflecting on the day that passed? Give yourself some time and be intentional about your daily reflection and how can you improve. What would it look like to take careful inventory of the first am thoughts and last pm thoughts? How do you open and close your day? How could you start today that would help to begin and end it well? This practice offers so many health benefits, one being better sleep.

If you are disappointed with something that took place in your day, write it down and place it in a jar. It is not yours to take to bed with you. Tomorrow is a new day. Correct or clarify if needed, and you can always circle back around tomorrow.

What can you do today that will make an impact on others' lives to cheer, to encourage them to excel, to celebrate them? We have journeyed a minute together in this book. Pause and think about what you have accomplished already working through this book. Have you devoted the time to growth you planned? What is in the way? What is no longer an issue you once faced when you started this book? Congratulations as you celebrate doing something as a reward for all your efforts and accomplishments.

Verse:

May the God of hope fill you with all joy and peace in believing, so that by the power of the Holy Spirit you may abound in hope.

~ ROMANS 15:13

Prayer:

Lord, thank you for the awareness I need to evaluate if I should hold on or let go. Today I choose to let it go. I place it into the jar of worries and concerns and give it to you. I no longer carry around the things that steal my joy, my sleep, and my peace. My need to have you in the center of my life does not give room to other dragging thoughts that weigh me down. I choose to live lighter, acknowledging you have it even when I don't see it yet. *Yet* is key and I thank you that I can worship you, pray to you, and give my burdens to you.

Gauge to Grow:

1. Think of three things that come to mind that need to be in the jar. What saddens your heart most? When convicted in an area what do you do to find a solution?

2. Think about all your committed steps going forward and list them. If your list does not line up and has you in a state of worry or concern, should you add this to the jar?

3. What fires you up? What lights up your face? What would bring you joy today? Celebrate and reflect on the steps you've taken, launching yourself forward in a new direction. Take a deep breath and ponder your growth. Think about who you were before starting this journey and where you are now. What can you add to the worry jar that you have no control over that is holding back your growth?

Week 33
Make a Move

Start this week reflecting on
three wins from last week.

The journey of a thousand miles begins with a single step.
~ Lao Tzu

Friends and loved ones can be miles apart yet heart-to-heart close relationally. Do you have a friend you wish you could see more or a family member? Take some time today to pray for them and write a letter of gratitude for having them in your life. Think about the ways they have impacted the way you think and the joy that their presence brings into your heart. Often times it's not the things that we say, it's the emotions we experience that linger for years to come.

Make a list of people who have had a great presence and made an impact in your life. Think about what they did specifically that helped move your life forward. Perhaps it was at a crucial time in your life, or they showed up to help when no one else was to be found to support you in your time of need. If you have been on the receiving end, you know how important a trusted friend can be in time of need. Let them know today. You never know what they are going through right now and how encouraging your letter could mean to them. My person is Sally, she passed away a few years ago. She took me under her wing and cared for me when I was so confused and alone. She allowed me to live with her and taught me healthy boundaries, how to love myself, and to appreciate my strengths and to laugh—truly laugh.

The importance of laughter cannot be overstated. To really enjoy life, find laughter daily. On very tough days Sally and I would just get in the car and drive. I remember particularly one day we drove in the snow to Cascade Locks and while on the road we came upon a car that had slid off the road into a ditch. We offered our winch to pull the car out. We continued on and discovered another family in need of help, and we continued assisting people all the way to Cascade Locks. Our own hurt and heartache were gone when we arrived. Helping all those people heal our hurting hearts, and we spoke about how stepping out to use what we had to help others is what it's all about. We discovered laughter and joy in serving and caring for those in need. We had a choice to help or to look down and stay isolated and sulking at home, alone. When you look up and see an opportunity, ask yourself, what do you have to share—to give and offer to others? When we're together with others, our perspective changes. That day we found healing. That day we were the answer to others' prayers. That day stopping to offer help we in turn received the help we so desperately needed. As I grew up and moved away, I would write her and let her know that I was thinking of her and was so grateful for her. I am so glad that I did.

Verse:

As each has received a gift, use it to serve one another, as good stewards of God's varied grace.

~ 1 PETER 4:10

Prayer:

Lord, help me to think of others and to step out and help those in need. Help me to be on the lookout for opportunities to care for others around me. Use my resources, strengths, gifts, and skills to be the answer someone is looking for when in need. Help me not to judge but to have the desire to care and serve along with others. Lord, thank you for allowing me the perspective of being other-minded. I pray you are seen in and through my life, as I commit to serve you in all I say and do. Amen.

Gauge to Grow:

1. Who is on your heart to reach out to? Reach out today to thank someone for being there for you in a difficult time.

2. What resources do you have that can be an answered prayer to someone else?

3. Make sure you are part of the reason someone does not stay stuck. List three ways you can offer help, three places to call to help and serve, and three people to do it with you.

Week 34

Perspective, Perspective, Perspective

· ·

Messages that give us feedback about life. Interruptions that should cause us to reflect and think. Signpost that directs us to the right path. Tests that push towards great maturity.
~ JOHN MAXWELL

We can complain or proclaim. It's a choice. In a season of brokenness, that's when He has our attention. When we don't have the answers, where we turn is vital to the outcome. Temporary vice or long-term blessings? It's in that moment of brokenness that we discover who we really are, where we want to be, and why.

What does your world look like? What is one decision you would like to make today to improve your circumstance? What will it take for things to look different? What do you need to do right now to implement change for the best positive result? We all process situations differently. Have you ever made a mistake? Well, today is your lucky day. Use it to gain perspective on how to process what not to do. This is a powerful avenue for growth. If we're not making mistakes we're not growing. Mistakes actually make growth possible.

Cultivate creativity and shove aside the obstacle of "What if it doesn't work?" Yes, what if it does? How about that? Then what? I read this on Facebook and thought I would share regarding perspective. Two young boys walked into a pharmacy one day, picked out a box of tampons, and proceeded to the checkout counter. The pharmacist at the counter asked the older boy, "Son, how old are you? "Eight," the boy replied. The man continued, "Do you know what these are for?" The boy replied, "Not exactly, but they are not for me. They're for him. He's my brother. He's four." "Oh really?" The pharmacist replied with a grin. "Yes," the boy said. "We both saw on TV that if you use these, you will be able to swim, play tennis, and ride a bike. Right now, he can't do none of those."

This story illustrates with humor the perspective and how knowing more can change your outcome.

Are you learning from your mistakes? Are you maturing? Do you notice how you are responding differently as situations arise? If not, opportunity will again arise in order to learn. Ask yourself, what can I learn from that situation and how can I grow? Lastly, what can I do next time to overcome?

My husband Chris and I argue every year about the Christmas tree. He is in no hurry to take it down when Christmas is over, and I find it practically offensive to see it still taking up space, with all the lights and ornaments for a holiday that is over. I hate arguing, though. I hate how I sound nagging and grinding when we have better things to talk about. So, this year I changed my perspective. This year I did something different. What did I say? NOTHING. Not a darn thing. I took all the ornaments off the tree and declared the tree was now for St. Patrick's Day. I decorated the tree full of green ornaments. It looked spectacular and not one conversation turned into a disagreement. We were on the same page because I chose to have a different perspective. Peace is primary. We need to learn to sacrifice in order to be a peacemaker and a peacekeeper. Too many things cause us to fight and take our peace. Home is our sanctuary. Do we treat it as such or is it a war zone? How can you cultivate a sanctuary atmosphere? Candles, music, good food, clean floors . . . hey, I didn't say it would be easy! Effort has benefits and so does laziness. How do you want your life to be marked? What do you want to be known for? With the tree up or down?

Verse:

For this light, momentary affliction is preparing for us an eternal weight of glory beyond all comparison, as we look not to the things that are seen but to the things that are unseen. For the things that are seen are temporary, but the things that are unseen are eternal.

~ 2 Corinthians 4:17–18

Prayer:

Lord, thank you for the perspective that in all I have gone through, you were there with me through it all. Not one thing I go through is without your awareness of it. Lord, we pray for right perspective, your perspective, as to not dwell on what was done to us but rather what you have done for us! Thank you, Lord.

Gauge to Grow:

1. What would happen if you looked at a given situation differently? If you don't like where you are right now, do something about it. What could you implement right now that would allow your perspective to improve?

2. Allow a different perspective to be seen in a situation that has you jaded. What can you learn from it?

3. Perspective is key. Is what you remember accurate and true? What can you pull out as a learned experience, from your perspective?

Comfort Zone

. . . .

Start this week reflecting on
three wins from last week.

Comfort zones are where dreams go to die.
~ REGINA KING

Bring clarity to your vision. Be specific with goals and
expectations and show up enthusiastically. Clarity regarding goals is pivotal. Anyone can have an idea, but it's what you
do with the idea that makes it tangible. Know that there will
be pushback once you establish goals. How will you handle it?
What will you do? Know who you are and what you are called
to do to make a difference.

Why does trouble always come knocking? I have asked myself
this question many times. Once we had a young gentleman who

came to us under the pretense of longing to be a part of our family and being a big brother to my three younger children. My husband and I had no idea that he had bad intentions toward my children and an appetite of a sinful nature, longing to entice our children for his own desires. Thankfully, God had sent my husband a dream, and for no reason I could articulate, I had a huge distaste for his company, and my heart shifted so that I did not want him around. I told my husband he was no longer welcome in my home. I had no reason for it. This young man was funny and polite. He was a student attending a well-known school in this area. My children all looked up to him as a big brother. But for some reason that I can't explain, I wanted to throat punch him. Now that sounds violent, and I've never felt like that prior to this point with this young man. As God would have it, things were revealed, and he is now serving seventeen years in prison.

Now we have two choices to make. Do we close off our family because we are skeptical of others' intentions? Do we no longer attend activities involving a well-known school in our area? No, this young man was struggling in sin and needed help. To put up boundaries would only be in the name of fear and cause unhealthy behavior as a reaction to one person and his wrong choices. So how do you trust again when you have been misguided or were taken advantage of? You go back to your family's vision and goals. I know this is a heavy topic; however, walking out difficulty when it stares you in the face lends itself to creating a life-giving season of growth in the Lord and depth in family.

I am here to tell you I have lived it. We have faced challenges as a family that we did not allow to define us but rather allowed us to grow closer as a family. One day at a time, one tear at a time, and one choice at a time, pressing in and pressing forward. Our family mantra is that people leave better when they came. We decided not to allow others over is to go against our family motto and what we stand for. No one and nothing can take that from us unless we give it. Nothing more was going to be taken from us. In our joy, our thoughts, and our memories, we chose not to allow ourselves to be tainted but to be gifted to be used somehow down the line in some way, using what took place to help others with compassion and insight experienced first hand. It's not just about what happens to you; it's also about what happens in you and how much energy and time you give it. That gives the offense power and will continue to wreak havoc if no clarity is obtained, or higher ground is sought. Solid ground that cannot be taken and shaken.

I had my moments for sure. I would be standing in the aisle at Target and get a call not knowing how I got there and why I was even there; I'd just be staring in a daze of almost disbelief. Give yourself time if something tragic has taken place in your life. However, time does not heal all wounds; it's what you do with your time that counts. Years down the road you could be nowhere close to healing but just rehearsing the situation over and over. Choosing to forgive and allow healing to take place have nothing to do with whether or not they deserve it. Rather, it has all to do with whether you deserve it. It's not your burden to bear. It does no good to allow one more second of hurt into your heart.

One good practice is to write it down and burn it. Another is to get a cross, write it down, and pin it to the cross. By acknowledging and releasing your emotions, you can unshackle yourself from the weight of past experiences. Recognize that Jesus Christ's sacrifice provides a path to healing, allowing you to let go of hurt and walk in freedom. Whatever that looks like for you, don't allow the shadow of the sin to be cast on you. Step out of the shadow into the light. Today is a new day and a new beginning in truth to hold on to living the dream that was meant for you. Important to note professional help is recommended in this area.

Verse:

A glad heart makes a cheerful face, but by sorrow of heart the spirit is crushed. The heart of him who has understanding seeks knowledge, but the mouths of fools feed on folly. All the days of the afflicted are evil, but the cheerful of heart has a continual feast. Better is a little with the fear of the Lord than great treasure and trouble with it.

~ Proverbs 15:13–16

Prayer:

Lord, we lift up all people hurting who are reading this. We remember that while this topic is heavy, Lord, you desire for our load to be light and our hurt to be lifted. We thank you for your clarity and your leadership in our life. Our minds are yours, our memories our yours, our life is yours, please breathe life-giving purpose into us once again as the knocking on our door grows quiet. We claim your peace, restful sleep at night, and the sense of purpose we have while living our lives every day. You have designed us to come together and care for one another. We are more powerful together than alone. We have more strength than weakness. We have words of truth flowing through our minds as we are being renewed. Help us to rest while you do the work. We are not the savior. Only you are, only you can set our feet on solid ground with a desire in our heart to renew our strength. We are at rest, we are restored, and we are redeemed in Jesus' name. Amen.

Gauge to Grow:

1. Be clear that no one or nothing can take your peace away from you.

2. What can you do today to show you are moving forward? What would it look like to show up with goals no one or nothing can steal? It's in your heart. You can't control what's in others' hearts.

3. What tangible desire do you have that has not been acted upon? How can you turn a disappointment into a victory statement?

4. How can you help someone else by drawing on what has happened to you or someone you love?

Core Values

. . . .

Start this week reflecting on
three wins from last week.

Most people don't want to be part of the process;
they just want to be part of the outcome. But the process is where
you figure out who's worth being part of the outcome.
~ SCOTTIE PIPPEN

If you could go back in time to fix or even erase all your past
mistakes, you'd be erasing yourself. Our mistakes are our
teachers and hence are a culmination of all life experiences.
Reframe past situations that made you grow. More than likely,
your most challenging times were what made you realize what
your core values were and that you had to respond according
to them. Perhaps it was in those situations that you discovered
you have a red line you refused to cross.

We see in scripture God changed a person's name at a dramatic, turning point of their life. Time after time, he changed a person's name at a dramatic turning point in their life story. Abram became Abraham, Saul became Paul, Jacob became Israel, and Simon became Peter. Their change of name corresponded with the change in their life. Each became unstoppable at fulfilling the purpose for which he was created, and the same is true for you. Which story are you telling about the pivotal moments in your life? Sometimes when we get stuck, getting unstuck does not necessarily involve rewriting your current script but rewriting the story we tell about our lives. If the story you tell leaves you as a victim, powerless, bitter, or helpless feeling, then it's time to change how you tell the story. What you say about your life in your circumstances is even more powerful than what others say. Think about the types of statement that keep you stuck. How do you tell the story of your challenges? What defensive statements do you make that label you in terms you don't actually want to describe you? What positive statements could you replace that you would want to describe your now and future self? What you say to yourself can either propel you forward or hold you back—and keep you looking back. Reframe any aspects of your story that leave you feeling disempowered tell the story in such a way that glorifies God and grows you.

The following examples are a great way to start. 1. Describe past challenges as events you have overcome, survived, or thrived in spite of. 2. Refuse to make anyone who hurt you the centerpiece of your story. They do not get the center stage in your story. Give God the starring role instead. 3. Describe the way in which your challenge grew you, enlightened you, protected you, or helped you through the situation. 4. Own any mistakes or failures you had. 5. List any good decisions you made and successes you had. 6. Tie your story to the present moment in a way that celebrates your resilience and unstoppable will. Consider for a moment the challenges or situations from your past you believe are holding you back somehow. This is also called a testimony. It's where you share what has taken place in your life and shift the negative attitude from self to how God brought you through a situation to the other side.

Verse:

On God rests my salvation and my glory; my mighty rock, my refuge is God. Trust in him at all times, O people; pour out your heart before him; God is a refuge for us. Selah.
~ PSALM 62:7–8

Prayer:

Lord, thank you for all I have gone through in my life. It has allowed me to overcome so many obstacles. I will not let the past define me, but I will rather allow your saving grace to redeem me. Thank you for the realization that in you my spirit is restored and allowed to thrive today like never before. Thank you so much for your love and free gift of right living in you. Amen.

Gauge to Grow:

1. If you were to tell the story using the six points above as a guideline, how would you tell the story differently?

2. Rewrite your script. What does your life look like when you are unstoppable?

3. Write a vivid description that inspires and energizes you.

4. Speak about the lessons you learned as you overcome your challenges and the opportunity it lent to you.

Week 37

Let Go of the Need to Control

. . . .

Start this week reflecting on
three wins from last week.

Control: Do you have it or does it have you?

*One of life's best coping mechanisms is to know the
difference between an inconvenience and a problem.*
~ ROBERT FULGHUM

hy might a person have controlling tendencies? The control
tendency shows up in a variety of ways like mood swings,
fear of abandonment, self-centeredness, possessiveness, a sense
of entitlement; a need to be the center of attention, a need to
have power and show it, jealousy, being easily agitated, having
unhealthy eating habits, difficulty accepting responsibility, and

lying. Things you can control and should control include your beliefs, your attitude, your thoughts, and your perspective. Symptoms review a heart hurt or an area that needs to be healed.

Experience is not what happens to you. Experience is what you do with what happens to you.
~ Aldous Huxley

How do you apply a new way of thinking that does not play into your insecurities that require not more control but release? How can this change increase your strength?

Ask yourself, where does this come from? What is the cause or the need to be in control? What are you defensive about? In what ways do you point the finger at others as an excuse for your controlling behavior? How does the need to control show up in your life? What would it look like to release the control? Name one area you can let go in. Just one, and be intentional about it. Notice the outcome when you do.

While I was in India, I was so hot and could not cool down. We had been out in the heat all day and regardless of shade or sun, this level of heat was so unbearable with no reprieve. I was getting irritated and wanted to just quit and go home. One day, we rested in a village where we were served food on banana leaves as we sat on a concrete floor. I was too hot and could not control anything around me. I was literally in the pits of despair wanting to go home. Right there you have a choice: how will I respond when upset? This is what I did . . . I set up three fold-up chairs under a tree and thought if I could just allow as much air around me as possible, perhaps it would be better. As I lay on my back across the three chairs I started to cry. I had no control over the weather, where we were going, and what to eat. I cried out to God and asked Him to just send a breeze of wind to cool me off so I could know He was with me, and I need not need to control anything but rest. As I was talking to God this amazing breeze rushed over me and I instantly felt cool but more so relieved that He cared for me and heard my heart's cry. As I opened my eyes, I noticed the leaves from the tree I was under was not moving. How can this be? Wind . . . Where was it coming from? I arched my head back and saw that a little girl was fanning me on my face then all over. That is when the tears really started to leak from my eyes. I spoke in Hindi thanking her and introducing myself. I knew in that moment that I did not need to be in control. God was right there with me, and I could rest. The heat and lack of control were no longer the issue as through His comfort he heard my cry, and I was blown away by His breeze.

Verse:

He delivered us from such a deadly peril, and he will deliver us. On him, we have set our hope that he will deliver us again. You also must help us by prayer, so that many will give thanks on our behalf for the blessing granted us through the prayers of many.

~ 2 CORINTHIANS 1:10–11

Prayer:

Lord, trust is found only in you. You alone are fully worthy to be praised. Take away all the anxious thoughts that swirl in my mind, confusing, and replace them with calm, clarity, and faith in you. When my heart is pounding and my head is swirling, help me to be aware of what is taking place and be grounded in you. Please forgive me for the times that I question you and complain about what is as I look forward to what is to come.

Gauge to Grow:

1. Where are you resisting or avoiding? How can you accept and relax? Name all the things you're grateful for. What are some ways you can retrain your brain to relax and replenish?

2. What pushes your buttons most? What are you grateful for most?

3. How can you lessen the frequency with which your buttons are pushed and grow in the area of self-control?

Week 38

Mothers

. . . .

Start this week reflecting on
three wins from last week.

*Why do we close our eyes when we pray, when we cry,
when we kiss, when we dream: because the most beautiful
things in life are not seen but felt by the heart.*

~ ANONYMOUS

To all the mothers out there . . .

When you become pregnant, no matter if you're full term or
have been pregnant only for a short amount of time, living cells
are exchanged. After the pregnancy, the cells will remain in your
body for the rest of your life. That is so amazing! Whether you
have experienced a miscarriage, no matter how long you've been

carrying your baby, the fact remains that the exchange of living cells has taken place, says PMC National Library of Medicine. FACT! That's amazing. We have the living cells of our mother in our body. "Mother intuition" could not be a truer phrase. Fetal cells migrate into the mother during pregnancy. Fetomaternal transfer pregnancy occurs in all pregnancies, and in humans, the fetal cells can persist for decades. Microchimeric fetal cells are found in multiple areas of the woman's body, including blood, bone marrow, skin, and liver. A small percentage of cells transfer from mother to fetus and fetus to mother.

Keelin O'Donoghue, PhD, MRCOG, says "The pregnancy-acquired low-grade chimeric state of women could have far-reaching implications, influencing recovery after injury or surgery, aging, graft survival after transplantation, survival after cancer as well as deciding the protective effect of pregnancy against diseases later in life. Lifelong persistence of fetal cells in maternal tissues may even explain why women live longer than men."

The physical exchange between baby and mother and mother and baby is phenomenal. Cells living and growing are bonded for life. Did you know that in breastfeeding women produce melatonin, the hormone of drowsiness, and higher levels of nucleotides thought to promote sleep? Breast milk pumped in the morning features higher concentrations of cortisol, a stress hormone that makes babies more alert. The detail even in breast milk production is orchestrated by the one who made both mother and child. This is only to add to the miracle of life. Life breathed in and out by our maker. It's a phenomenon, one to ponder and embrace.

Verses:

Yet she will be saved through childbearing—if they continue in faith and love and holiness, with self-control.

~ 1 Timothy 2:15

Behold, children are a heritage from the Lord, the fruit of the womb a reward.

~ Psalm 127:3

Before I formed you in the womb I knew you, and before you were born I consecrated you.

~ Jeremiah 1:5a

Prayer:

Lord, we thank you that you are the giver of life. Your word says that you know our first breath and you know our last. Lord, we thank you for the blessing of being called mothers and daughters. Thank you for our mothers, maternal and paternal. We know that you created us for life to flourish in and through our minds, our mouths, and our lives. Lord, help all that we say and do and everything that comes from us to be glorifying to you. Thank you for allowing our mothers to carry us, who even after birth still carry us. Thank you for your design. Thank you for allowing our moms to care for us to the best of their ability. We pray for them now and thank you for the gift of motherhood, Lord. We thank you for the process that takes place inside of our body and for the miracle of life you allow us to live. Lord, we pray for words of healing, hope, and the grace to proclaim your holiness. Let that be the evidence of our life in Jesus' name. Amen.

Gauge to Grow:

1. How has this healing truth given you peace and strength today?

2. How does this apply to your life?

3. In what way is this freeing to you? How can this help you in the future? Take some time to talk about and write about all the benefits this lends to your life. How does it show up in your mother-and-child relationship?

Take away: be chill, babies feed off you more than you know . . .

Week 39
Life Isn't Fair

. . . .

Start this week reflecting on
three wins from last week.

*In a world full of opinions, let us remember, the
truth that matters most is not of this world.*
~ ELIZABETH SPENNER

As an elementary teacher, do you know how many times I
have heard this said on any given day, that "life isn't fair"?
And the statement is true. We want fairness, and we also want
that which is right, true, and good. However, that's not the way
in this world. How can we reframe this statement? How can this
unfairness of life be a positive to both you and me? To take it
a step further, we might even be glad that life is not fair. What
does fair look like to you? What have you been given that you

did not deserve? How do you respond when it's not fair in your favor and when you are grateful life is not fair and you have gained more than you deserve? Notice your knee-jerk reactions. Do you clam up, point fingers, stomp your feet, demand to settle the score, and make things right? Or do you see it as a character-building opportunity? When a situation does not sit right and you feel the frustration inside you building up, take a deep breath and see it for what it is: an opportunity to see things from a different angle. Our vision can be obstructed if we remain seated where we are currently. This is precisely when your true self appears, and your real character is seen. Developed or undeveloped, this rub is the opportunity to see what area is your strength or what area you can grow in, given this opportunity.

Living a life with no regrets, as to not miss any more opportunity and to see the aggravation with ease. How can I say that? When emotions run high, do you find your sound judgment is obscured? What to do? Options include walking away, praying, or staying and speaking with grace. You can rest in grace knowing you don't have all the facts, and in knowing things might look different twenty-four hours from now or a week from now. There is power in the pause. Cultivate grace in believing the way you show up right now might not be about you. It might be just what someone needs to see in order to see hope, be heard, and experience being cared for. What does that look like?

I have regretted speaking before thinking of the other person first. Have you done that too? I mean, I speak sometimes when I should be quiet, for you can't unsay words after they're spoken. "I want what's fair" was all I might be thinking about, not the other person, and I was not representing well the One I proclaim to have living in me as my Lord and Savior. I know I ought always to be living an example out of the abundance of love I've received from our Lord and Savior, but it's a process. When we elevate ourselves, we justify the value system in our hearts at the cost of hurting others. There is a cost to that. "For out of the abundance of the heart the mouth speaks." How do you respond when buttons are pushed, triggers are pulled, and fears are exposed? What would it look like to take a deep breath and walk out with the big picture in mind? Here's an option: remember to be kind to yourself and know when it's just too much at that moment to process. Learning to be self-aware, ask yourself what emotion you are experiencing and why? Should you respond the way you're thinking of responding? Do you have a measured response to the situation? Give yourself a choice about how to respond and walk through different outcomes in your mind. Would more information allow clarity in this situation so it could make more sense? Retraining takes noticing and evaluating a desired change. Desire to make the change, take steps to change, then be the change.

The choices, repercussions, and benefits of growth are at hand. When would be a good time to add or diffuse the situation? Space means you know yourself to be true to yourself and will not get lost in the confusion or emotion of the situation. Having proper self-evaluation is key.

At first, when I was starting this retraining of my thoughts, I would do the opposite of how I feel. I realized just because I feel it does not make it true. Retraining the mind takes making a mental shift and then thinking about the possible best outcome.

If what has been done has not worked in the past, to continue to respond in the same manner is foolish. So, what if we were to try the opposite of how you responded in the next situation?

Are you able to do that? Are you able to keep a silent watch over your heart so as to not get derailed, again? If you get stuck, how do you get unstuck? You have been given this time on earth for a unique purpose. We are counting on you to fulfill that purpose. Wisdom is to utilize the pause, no longer wanting what's fair but what's best!

Verse:

For the mouth speaks what the heart is full of. A good man brings good things out of the good stored up in him, and an evil man brings evil things out of the evil stored up in him. But I tell you that everyone will have to give account on the day of judgment for every empty word they have spoken. For by your words, you will be acquitted, and by your words, you will be condemned.

~ MATTHEW 12:34B–37

Prayer:

Lord, help me to take a deep breath and know that fair is not the life for me. Your best is what you have promised. Help me not to be short-sighted but trust you in the big picture. You see it all from my first breath to my last breath. You have control when even in the moment all seems too out of control and uncertainty is at my doorstep. You are the maker of the universe. Nothing is too difficult for you. Help me to keep that in perspective when dealing with my life as I walk out well when life deals with me. Help me to see it as an opportunity, not an annoyance. Thank you for the perspective that is outside of my narrow thinking. For your thoughts are so beyond my thoughts and your ways beyond my ways. I love you. I trust you. Today more than yesterday. Amen.

Gauge to Grow:

1. What steps can you take today to see perceived unfairness for what it is, a chance for character building and growth?

   Instead of selfish how do we become selfless? Prepare for the opportunity for it will come to see growth. Training for the life test starts today for the best outcome tomorrow.

2. What would it look like to read your bible for fifteen minutes, starting in Matthew working your way through the whole bible? What do you have to lose? What do you have to gain? Renewing your mind takes intention. Remember, it's not about the time it's about the habit that formulates the longevity of character.

3. When quieting your spirit for five minutes of distraction-free time to speak and be spoken to, what has taken place in your life? How do you know if it's you or God? I have heard it said it enters your thoughts and you know it's too good to have come from you. When you dream vividly, write your dream down along with any thoughts that enter your mind.

Making daily steps is going in the right direction. Recognize what you are committing to, be aware what is being awakened within your spirit and move forward into a healthy thought life.

Week 40

Rainbows and Rain

. . . .

Start this week reflecting on
three wins from last week.

Behind this mountain is more mountains.
~ OLD PROVERB

We all have days where it's rainbows and other days it's
rain. Both are needed; in order to see the rainbow we
need rain. To overcome this, we need to push back our adversity to allow growth to occur. Stop and observe what you see.
Learning to dance in the rain and not wish it away as rain is
needed for the rainbow to appear. There will be days to forget,
days to remember, and days to savor. Every decision made in
the day sets the tone for the next and culminates in feelings,
decisions, and progress toward the next goal. Where you are

today is a culmination of thoughts, decisions, and days lived and experienced. Take some time now to evaluate where you are and where you want to be. What thoughts do you have? Is it positive or negative? Are you stuck in an unpleasant past or are you visualizing a flourishing future? What are you preparing for in these mental dress rehearsals? If things don't seem to go the way you imagined, how can you give the benefit of the doubt in the meantime?

Celebrate memories, choosing to rehearse positive memories, choices, and decisions you have made—big or small, it matters. You are living, breathing, and moving. Some choices you have made are short lived and others are long lasting. This is called a growth mindset or fixed mindset. How you look at the situation will determine your next move. None of us are perfect. Allow growth opportunities to be just that and give grace to yourself and others in their growth journey. If you wish you had made a different choice, ask yourself what you have learned from this situation, turn from that road, and take a different one that leads to the life you picture in your mind's eye. A fixed mindset will say this is always what people do or that you will never trust again because this person just did this or that. "I always do this" is another, along with, "What's the use, it's no point trying?" When it's an isolated situation, we make that isolated situation into a learning opportunity and take what we need from that moment to grow. A fixed mindset is absolutist, involving the belief that nothing will change, so why bother? Ask yourself if you have an area in your life that you have an isolated, fixed mindset about, or do you have a growth mindset about it?

What it's all about? By Roy Lessin

It's not about following your career path; it's about following His call upon our lives.

~ MATTHEW 16:24

It's not about our self-efforts to live for Him; it's about letting Him live His life in us.

~ GALATIANS 2:20

It's not about our attempts at self-improvement; it's about His transforming grace.

~ 2 CORINTHIANS 5:17

It's not about our self-image; it's about being conformed to His image.

~ ROMANS 8:29

It's not about our abilities to serve; it's about His power to equip us.

~ ACTS 1:8

It's not about our human resources; it's about His sufficiency.

~ 2 CORINTHIANS 3:5

It's not about wanting the approval of others; it's about having His approval.

~ 2 TIMOTHY 2:15

Verse:

Do nothing from selfish ambition or conceit, but in humility count others more significant than yourselves. Let each of you look not only to his own interests but also to the interests of others.

~ PHILIPPIANS 2:3–4

Prayer:

Lord, today is the day I am asking you to help me grow in my heart to expand my understanding of you and the week ahead. Help me to breathe in your goodness and exhale the insecurities that come from wrong thinking. I ask you to help me be aware of toxic thoughts. Thank you for your Word of truth that I can trust and that gives assurance of the steady path I am on. Steady my steps, bringing me to the Cross as I revive your love for me. Thank you, for that love that is given just for me. Grow me up as I look up. Amen.

Gauge to Grow:

1. How do you respond when you are hurt, rejected, or disappointed?

2. Journal and have an accountability friend or life coach to hold you accountable.

3. How often do walls come up to deflect potential hurt? Be mindful of automatic thoughts. Are they true?

4. There is no one else like you in this world. So what are you going to do about it? Smile like you mean it, and lean into the dream that only you have in your heart. Take a step today toward it and watch hope and purpose unfold.

Communication Tools

. . . .

Start this week reflecting on
three wins from last week.

By failing to prepare you are preparing to fail.
~ Benjamin Franklin

How do you know the right tool to communicate properly?
As you enter this topic, think about your desire to bring
clarity to the conversation, and remember that conversation has
a purpose that requires effective communication to be reached.

What is a text for? What is a phone call for? What is worth a
face-to-face conversation and what is email worthy? Talk about
your thoughts or ideas before moving on. How do you use them?
Are you using the right communication medium?

Text: This great tool is used every day. This is best used when communicating short bits of facts, a list of items, a reminder, a quick note (thinking of you), or a note to reach out to set a time to talk or get together. I'm sure you can think of more.

Phone conversation: Appropriate when you need to talk more than you can in a quick text, and you want to communicate more on a feelings level with tone included and you desire an immediate response. Through the phone, you can share on a heart-to-heart level your thoughts, feelings, and ideas.

E-mail: Good for documenting, working, and keeping a formal transaction record needed to file and keep for further reference.

I'm sure you could think of a few more good reasons for each. So what happens when we text or snap when we should have made a phone conversation or Facetime call? Miscommunication. So much is said nonverbally or with many sliding variables. Did I have a bad day at work? Was our last conversation not so great? Was that sarcasm? What's the tone? What face is she making? Am I saying this in a negative voice, or perhaps this is not the voice at all they are using over text? Pause before you reach out.

Ask yourself, "Is this an appropriate time to reach out?" Typically, after 9 am or before 9 pm is a good rule of thumb unless something else has been agreed upon. What are some other things you could think of here regarding time? Is this appropriate information to share in a group chat? Is this beneficial to all receiving this information? Do they want to receive this information? How is this conversation helpful?

What is the purpose of sharing this text? Do I seem to just share about myself and my point of view all the time? When

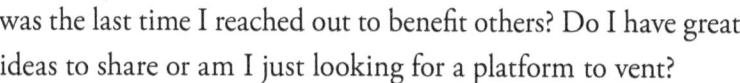

was the last time I reached out to benefit others? Do I have great ideas to share or am I just looking for a platform to vent?

This brings me to Facebook. What are some healthy ways to use Facebook? Have you seen Facebook benefit others?

Much is shared on Facebook that would have been better in a diary or a journal. I call this diarrhea of the mouth. Where a filter and self-control would be best, political declarations are made and venting erupts, resulting in severed relationships. Much more is shared behind the veil of a screen than face to face. Consequent hurt transpires without accountability.

How is Facebook a tool for good? Facebook is a great tool for staying connected with people far away, to advertise a service you enjoy or that you yourself offer, or to share ideas, events, and activities. List some ways it's used well as a guideline for future use. What else comes to mind that could benefit? Is anything coming to mind that needs to be addressed? How can you tell if you are using the wrong vehicle to communicate? If you find yourself saying, "That's not what I meant," then perhaps a different vehicle is needed. Clarity is essential. Connivance is not productive and can have long-lasting negative effects.

I experienced this firsthand when I received the news via text that my godmother had passed by a phone call while I was out shopping. Ask if this is a good time to talk? Allow the other person grace if they are in the middle of something to have them call you back when it's a better time to share. Emotional topics have powerful effects on our bodies. When sharing a deep, heartfelt conversation, allow the communication of care and other mindedness. Wait for the right time when a person can be in a safe place to receive sad information in a private setting.

Other-mindedness will give the opportunity to grow when you are in a difficult time. It's not just about the information; the conversation will open up the way toward a deepening of the relationship when done properly in both respect to time and to the vehicle used to converse.

Another incident that comes to mind is when I learned some terrible news on social media that concerned a close friend of mine, something she didn't know yet, and as her friend, I knew I needed to be there and tell her personally. I drove to her house, shared, held her, and we cried together. I hated the fact that it had to be done, but we were together face to face, and the blow was cushioned because it had been delivered with love.

Verse:

Then the Lord spoke to you out of the midst of the fire. You heard the sound of words but saw no form: there was only a voice. And He declared to you His covenant, which He commanded you to perform, that is, the Ten Commandments, and He wrote them on two tablets of stone.

~ DEUTERONOMY 4:12–14

Prayer:

Lord, thank you for all the means we have to care for others and the responsibility to do so in love and effectiveness. We pray for wisdom and the power to speak with care and love to others. Help us to be other-minded, offering solutions, and not becoming the problem. Help us to be good stewards of the lives you put in our path. May we continually look to you as you care so deeply for us and have given us your Word in the Bible. You speak to us in prayer all the time. We thank you that you are a personal God. Help us to speak from that place. Amen.

Gauge to Grow:

1. How could good communication benefit you in the future?

2. List all the pros and cons. Do you think any adjustment is needed?

3. What can you do to implement this change if change is needed?

4. Write down a time this was done right in your life and a time it could have been improved upon. What did you learn?

Week 42

Breakthrough

. . . .

Start this week reflecting on
three wins from last week.

*Management is about persuading people to do things they
do not want to do. While leadership is about inspiring
people to do things they never thought they could.*
~ STEVE JOBS

o you believe it? Have you seen it? Are you ready? What
has you stuck in doubt and hesitation? What would it
look like to experience a breakthrough? Picture yourself on the
other side of the breakthrough. Write about the scenario. What
benefits does it allow? Who will you be able to help? What can

you do today to cultivate clarity about a question in need of clarity? What have you done to prepare for future growth and expansion? How have you set yourself up for the best possible outcome? How are you managing yourself on the daily? What could you improve by spending five minutes helping to elevate you to your best?

I discovered one of the biggest, longest seasons of growth and becoming the best version of myself when I had someone accuse me of something I did not do nor would have ever done. The accusations went on for seven years but the whole time I stayed true to my character, allowed my life to speak volumes, and learned how to quiet my soul when wronged. My husband took a job working for a year and a half in Boston but was home with me in NY on the weekends. I also experienced much personal loss as my godmother, my father-in-law, and my brother-in-law all passed. It just seemed like a very short time, so I had to adjust my perspective and rest in the truth. Certain realizations helped me through this tough time:

1. I was innocent. I was accused but not convicted.

2. I will see my loved ones in heaven.

3. My husband being away was not forever. He contracted for a year and a half, not forever.

We can pump our fist, demand our way, or take the higher ground less traveled and allow our life to glorify God our Lord and maker.

I thought about what brings me joy daily: working with kids and serving at church. So, I went Friday night and started serving at the youth group in my church. I decided I did not like doing dishes, so we started using paper plates—don't judge me! I decided to go to Oregon for the weekend for the funeral of my godmother and was asked to speak. This gave me time to reflect on how grateful I was for her love and care in my life and allowed me to shift my perspective from what I could not fix to what I could do with the time gifted me. I could stay home miserable or invest in others and know this too shall pass. Who will I be on the other side of this?

Verse:

Let your eyes look directly forward, and your gaze be straight before you. Ponder the path of your feet; then all your ways will be sure. Do not swerve to the right or to the left; turn your foot away from evil.

~ PROVERBS 4:27

Prayer:

Lord, I give you my thoughts, my heart, and my dreams. Please close the gaps as I reach for the next desired outcome. Give me peace in my spirit and allow unsettling to occur in my heart when it's not your will. I need you to guide and direct me. Help me in all the areas that I need to let go of so I can grab ahold of you. Thank you for being all that I need. I love you, Lord.

Gauge to Grow:

1. How would others describe your positive qualities?

2. How can you improve your strengths?

3. How can you lend a hand to someone in need?

4. Who looks up to you?

5. Are you in the way of growth? What is holding you back?

6. Have you prayed about it? What verses pertain to what you are wrestling with? Write them out.

Week 43

Control Part 2

. . . .

Start this week reflecting on
three wins from last week.

He who controls others may be powerful,
but he who has mastered himself is mightier still.
~ Lao Tzu

Oftentimes we focus on what we can't control. Here are some suggestions regarding areas in your life that you can control. Focus your mind on what you can control and the things you cannot control will become smaller.

What can you do often? What do you have control over? What are you grinding on that takes the joy of your day away? What do you learn when you give up control?

Your perspective, your beliefs, your thoughts, your self-talk, your attitude, your friends, your books, your plans, your thoughtfulness—with all your resources, reach out and help someone else. How do you perceive situations? Negatively or positively? How often do you communicate care? How often do you say, "I love you"? How often do you say, "Thank you"? How authentically do you express positive feelings? Do you choose to ask for help? Do you regularly have an attitude of gratitude? How do you perceive others, positively or negatively? Do you give the benefit of the doubt to others? On a scale of 1–10 how often do you allow others in? How long does it take to get up after you've been knocked down? How much do you appreciate the lessons learned while you were down? How long does it take you to look up, reach up, and go up? In our tribe, we don't usually go through the hard times of life at the same time. We need to value others in their time of need. Thankfully, when life happens it's to teach us; we decide what we learned. If you have not trusted the process yet or have attained this lesson, the time is now. Learn from the buffalo: they instinctively run into the eye of the tornado, charging it head-on and saving their life by running smack dab in the middle of the storm. How many times we do run only to be clobbered? Learn the lesson: allow instinct to rise and fear to take the back seat.

My friend is a wonderful woman of faith and has an amazing husband and son. Her courage and drive are unmatched. Over seventeen years ago, her husband suffered a brain illness, putting him in a coma for a year and with regular seizures that have continued. Against all odds, he walks to the best of his ability (with a walker) but is unable to communicate. His ability to speak was taken from him in a surgery gone horribly wrong.

If anyone has a reason to shake their fist at God, it's their family. Unfair? Limitations? Wrong? He had been a thriving pastor, teacher, and missionary all over the world. Their life now is a much different one than the one they had planned. Yet every week, he chooses not to look at what limitations he has but at the capability he does have to get up early every Sunday ready to be taken to church and raise his crippled hand up to the Lord in worship. He has control over how he responds to this life he must now live differently but still to the best of his ability to the Glory of God. This man leads his family well in integrity, faithfulness, and love. We pray and believe in healing this side of heaven.

Many friends and family gather to support them as his strong, loving wife for life and son stand by his side. Recently, she was diagnosed with brain cancer. Again, I watched her go into New York City to receive treatment, blood transfusions, and chemo. A cascade of emotions flooded her heart as she let go of her hair, her control, and her strength. We have spoken at length, and I have seen a strength rise up in her no one could muster using only their earthly powers. The doctors call her miraculous. Miraculous is her new name. She chose to rest in the miraculous and receive healing, and now she no longer has cancer. It's over, it's gone—all scans are clear. Will her hair grow back? Yes. Will her job be there for her when it's time for her to return? Yes. But who she is returning to is no longer with a known limited perspective. Her perspective has grown and is deeper, and she is more patient. When asked, she is a better version of who she was meant to become. They are a powerhouse couple. The blessing outweighs the limited perspective of mere earthly happiness. She has tasted heaven, she has been at her end, and in the end, she started living—really living. She treasures people in her life like never before, has discovered strength like never before, and has let go of control like never before. And she is aware of what truly matters when all is stripped away, with hands raised, open, and ready to receive.

Are your hands raised? Are you ready to receive it today? Not in the way you may be picturing it, all wrapped up in a perfect bow. Do we shake our fists, blame God, and curse Him? What awaits at each extreme? How are you on the other side of what you are walking through? Bitter or better? Beautiful or beaten? Victim or victorious?

Verse:

The purpose in a man's heart is like deep water, but a man of understanding will draw it out.

~ PROVERBS 20:5

Prayer:

Lord, we thank you that we are not in control and that you are. Lord, in you, we trust the outcome, and we trust the process. Lord, I thank you. With open hands, we choose to receive your goodness and grace, no matter if it looks that way from our limited perspective or not. Lord, we choose to be victorious. We choose to be beautiful and we choose to be better—better than we were yesterday, more beautiful in the eyes of our beholder, and more victorious than we imagined we could be. Lord, thank you for all that you are doing and continue to do in our life. In you we trust, in you we rest, and in you we have hope.

Gauge to Grow:

1. If you have lost someone dear, it's hard to breathe and difficult to live with the loss. What joy did you experience together? How were you shaped by the joy experienced in the relationship?

2. How do you worship God to the best of your ability till you meet again? How can you be there for someone else who needs to know they are not alone?

3. Consider delivering food or serving in some other way, in a manner you yourself were the recipient during a trying time in your own life. Could this provide healing for your heart? What can you do today to start living to honor your loved one well?

Sisterhood Support

· ·

Start this week reflecting on
three wins from last week.

Each friendship represents a world in us,
a world not born until they arrive, and it's only
by this meeting that a new world is born.

~ ANAÏS NIN

Sister Beams is a construction term called "joist sistering."
It's the key to repairing floors through a process known as
sistering. This process involves attaching a new joist alongside
an existing joist to increase its strength.

Do you provide strength? Would anyone claim that you are
great at sistering? On a scale of 1 to 10, how do you show up
for others to support them? This is something I have pondered

for quite some time. Have you ever noticed how a person can share about a time in their life that was hard, discouraging, and even devastating, and in that moment, you can relate and find yourself all the sudden not so alone, and even a friend to the one sharing the memory, providing support in that precise moment in time when it was so needed?

There in a vulnerability, a transparency, involved in knowing it did not define you but allowed a closeness to be experienced by making the secret hurt in your heart no longer hidden.

It's the sense of support that comes from knowing I'm not alone. You feel the pain and joy in a shared memory, knowing it's not who you are. It was a just temporary moment in time you experienced. And when we choose to share it with others, the secret of silence is revealed and released. The grip no longer has a hold anymore. When brought to light, it has the power to be a sisterhood secret of sincerity discovered, allowing support as we come alongside each other to tend to a vulnerable area of the heart. It then has the power to be a strength. Friendships are revealed in a moment. To hear someone say, "I thought I was the only one!" has the power to bring relief as we discover friends in adversity. Sisterhood, too, is discovered in the secret moments of our lives when we choose to share.

We admire one another, lift up one another, and celebrate the reality that, though we may not be there any more, we are comforted nonetheless in knowing that we are not alone in this journey of life. Soul sister, kindred spirit, or sisterhood—whatever we call it, we strive to use the journey as steppingstones, not stones to be thrown, and on that journey, we leverage each other. I have two friends who do this so well. They are genuine and after a conversation, they ask questions about your personal life and offer help to levitate your plate every time. That is what they are known for: being caring, lifting, and encouraging friends. You walk away refreshed and grateful for their friendship every time.

What have you walked through that is holding you down or holding you back? What did you learn? Who can you share with to help them in what they are walking through? How can your experience help by leveraging others for support? What is the secret that someone can hold a flashlight for you to illuminate the dark place that, when light is shined on it, becomes a source of strength?

Take some time and develop the way you frame that hurtful time of your life to help someone.

You are not the victim; you are an overcomer! The situation is proof that you overcame adversity and cultivated [fill in the blank] because of it. Care, compassion, kindness, forgiveness you never thought was possible, and deeper relationship with others and Christ.

Never forget three types of people in your life: those who were there for you in difficult times, those who left you in difficult times, and those who contributed to your difficult times. History will repeat itself unless you break the cycle. Ask yourself what you can learn from this situation. If you see a repetitive pattern, do the opposite. You are who you attract. If you are attracting gossip, stepping out of the pattern of listening will often silence the negativity. What is done to you can be used to help others through you. This is the final stage of healing when you are able to help someone else walk through a similar circumstance.

Be the friend you wish you'd had.

You can become bitter or better. When better, you rise; with bitter, you repeat. If you allow bitterness to win, you will have rendered yourself ineffective. You step out of the race and disqualification is your tombstone. People will say things that hurt, and people will treat you unfairly. Life is hard-hitting and the hits will keep coming. What your personal perspective is and how you process are crucial. When we expect all to go well, we set ourselves up for perfection. When perfect is no longer a reality, we crumble and can lose hope. If every time we are disappointed in others, our perspective will be that "people can't be trusted." You told yourself a now-personal "truth" that the value of people is less than and not worth your time and energy. Not long after, your perspective on others could lead to discouragement and despair. We then start to criticize, devalue, and become less likely to care for others for fear of frustration and self-preservation. Where will that take you? Walk it out? Is that really how you want it to go?

We are wired to avoid discomfort. When we are stretched but enter into a situation with the intention of investing in our neighbor, then we are truly serving the way Christ calls us to. Let's go back to sistering. It's a construction term denoting a process used to support another floor joist that needs support. A sister beam, analogously, is when we come along in a struggle and lend a supportive friendship. This is a benefit to you as your peace will automatically increase. Ask yourself, what shifted? Did your attention shift? Could a changed outlook come from all the wrongs done to you and realizing that now it's about others and showing up when they hurt? If you are longing for sistering to take place in your life, look for a sistering opportunity. You can't have what you do not possess and are not willing to give.

Verses:

I do not turn aside from your rules for you have taught me. How sweet are your words to my taste, sweeter than honey to my mouth! Through your precepts I get understanding; therefore I hate every false way. Your Word is a lamp to my feet and a light to my path.

~ Psalm 119:102-105

The secret things belong to the Lord our God, but the things that are revealed belong to us and to our children forever, that we may do all the words of this law.

~ Deuteronomy 29:29

To you, O God of my fathers, I give thanks and praise, for you have given me wisdom and might, and have now made known to me what we asked of you, for you have made known.

~ Daniel 2:23

Prayer:

Lord, we thank you for friendship, for allowing us the opportunity to be fully known and fully cared for. Help me to care for others you have placed into my life. I pray for a thicker skin. Lord, I need it. No one is perfect and I am not even close. With this thick skin, I pray for offenses not to be noticed and for forgiveness to be quickened in my heart. Help me to care for people as they are and for you to transform as only you can.

I thank you ahead of time for the oversight for others, for the grace needed, and for the grace given. Help me to embrace your goodness, your faithfulness in friendships, and the desire to grow in them. I lift up my friends and what they are going through today. In Jesus' Name. Amen.

Gauge to Grow:

1. Think about what areas you have grown in friendship.

2. What have you walked through that could help someone else?

3. How could this help in the future?

4. How can your experience help leverage others?

5. What is the secret that could hold a flashlight for others?

6. Anyone you know of in need? Write out a card, make a meal, and offer to babysit, and clean.

7. What are qualities that you possess today that you can give to make or encourage a friend?

Week 45

Cultivating Daily Habits

. . . .

Start this week reflecting on
three wins from last week.

*The driver on the highway is safe not when he
reads the sign but when he obeys them.*
~ AW TOZER

Habits that reinforce identity are good habits, negative habits that conflict with your identity, not so much!

Create a habit awareness list. As you create your habit list, there is no need to change any of your habits at first. The reason for this exercise is to be aware of the habits that you are cultivating and determine if they are benefiting you or not. Observe your thoughts and actions without judgment or internal criticism.

Just ask yourself why you do what you do. Does it serve you or are you unaware of the habit you have created? We create and then hold on to our habits, not processing the why behind them. Make a detailed list and evaluate if any given habit is serving the purpose of becoming the person you desire to become.

When entering your house, ask yourself if you are hungry? What healthy food did you prepare before leaving the house? If none is prepared, make a mental note to prepare a healthy meal in the evening so you are set up for the next day. Do it when you are not in need and desperate. Desperate cravings result in shortcuts with long-term disappointments. When we make a decision based on emotions or with a wing-it attitude, regret and consequences are the payment for that quick fix.

So do it when your will is strong. Ask yourself, will this food help me reach my desired goal? What will happen if I eat this? Chances are, if you prepare ahead of time, it's a good choice and you will eat knowing you are serving your body and desired goal. Feelings shouldn't be the driving force when willpower is weak. Let's face it: hourly and daily we fluctuate. We must consciously choose to set ourselves up for positive outcomes in the days and weeks to come.

Back to your habit list. Put a plus (+) sign if it's a positive habit, a minus (-) sign if it's not beneficial for reaching your desired goal, an asterisk (*) if it has multiple benefits, and an equal (=) sign if neutral.

When I'm hungry, do I make poor choices? Before bed how is my willpower? When in the day is my cut-off time to eat/do I have a cut-off time? Should I? How would this benefit you to set healthy boundaries to help strengthen your willpower and avoid poor choices? You might set up healthy options for meals the day before. This will serve your pocketbook too. Willpower is strong power. Retrain your brain to use food to serve you, not you serve the food. Set yourself free from being a slave to your belly. I have heard it said: "eat to live not live to eat." It's right thinking to habitually avoid unhealthy living. Just a thought: try to drink a cup of room temp or slightly cold water before or while eating. The National Academy of Medicine suggests an adequate intake of daily fluids of about thirteen cups. Another finding is from the National Academy of Science, Engineering, and Medicine, which recommends an average daily water intake of about 125 oz for men and about 91 oz for women. That's 15.6 cups daily. Listen to your body and ask yourself what your body needs. What healthy choices am I making this week that will help me achieve the outcome I desire? Who am I teaching my healthy choice to? Who else will benefit from this self-aware for longevity of life care?

Verse:

That the God of our Lord Jesus Christ, the Father of glory, may give you the Spirit of wisdom and of revelation in the knowledge of him, having the eyes of your hearts enlightened, that you may know what is the hope to which he has called you, what are the riches of his glorious inheritance in the saints, and what is the immeasurable greatness of his power toward us who believe, according to the working of his great might.

~ EPHESIANS 1:17–19

Prayer:

Lord, help me to make daily choices that will help me physically, mentally, and emotionally. I need the brand-new perspective that will come from knowing you are guiding me daily in making good choices that will allow my body to live well from the daily food choices I make. I thank you for all the blessings you have given me. I thank you for this body you have given me to steward well. Help me more this week to set myself up the day before, reaping the benefits of how you have wired my body to function. Help me not to take them for granted and serve you well in all that I say and do. I thank you for bringing this area of my life under your authority. I give you my will and my ways. Help me to seek your wisdom in my daily choices this week. Amen.

Gauge to Grow:

1. Ask yourself, who is it that I am desiring to become?

2. What are some negative habits that have become daily routines? The more positive habits get put on autopilot, the better, since that allows us to learn new techniques and grow.

3. Think three steps ahead. What can I prep and plan for three steps ahead that will serve me and my family well? This will lessen stress and cultivate health in what I choose to ingest.

The Three-Minute Rule

. . . .

Start this week reflecting on
three wins from last week.

Compare yourself to who you were yesterday,
not to who someone else is today.
~ JORDAN PETERSON

This takes being intentional. The easier it is to continue a
habit, the more likely you are to continue. Think about
the areas you desire to grow in for a balanced lifestyle in body,
soul, and mind.

Body: What would it look like to show up every morning and
do three minutes of core work every day? Showing up is the first
and best step. What would it take to add a minute each week?
Focus primarily on this week till you have mastered the three

minutes. If you miss a day, start over. Do three minutes for five days, then next week go to four minutes till you have mastered that week. It's about showing up and being committed to the work that day. Pick a routine that works for you. I have dice for my gym class that I roll to see whether we will do sixty seconds of burpees, squats, crunches—the list goes on. This makes it fun. How can you incorporate fun into your workout?

What motivates you? A song to dance to, line dancing, piano music, hip-hop? Be creative. This will make it tangible and easy to repeat, causing endorphins to be released and creating the likelihood you'll return the next day. When we focus on the win and show up, the results will follow in the long run.

Soul: How would praying for three minutes every day benefit you? Show up each morning, have a place you enjoy to pray up, and start praying for ninety seconds and listen for ninety seconds. Train your brain to just be still. This allows you to enter the day with a clear head and heart. Apply additional minutes as described above.

Mind: Last but not least. Read the Bible every morning, starting with three minutes daily. Think about the benefits as you walk out the door to enter your day. The Bible is full of instruction and wisdom. Learn to love what will help line your mind up better. What could that do to jump-start your day? When is the day you are going to start? Evaluate after a week how this new habit is helping. Apply the additional minutes as described for the body.

Another idea to check out is coupling for the thirty-minute rule option. Pay attention to how long you are on your phone checking social media like Facebook. Have a designated location coupled with a positive desire to form new habits that will help you reach your goals. For example, when doing cardio, that is when you can check Facebook, Instagram or Snapchat. When watching something or listening to a podcast, watch thirty minutes of it while folding laundry. A well-established habit based on positive reinforcement from the enjoyment you get from the activity (like exercise) sets you up to achieve a long-term goal that might have seemed out of reach due to it being perceived as difficult and undesirable. If you look forward to the activity, you'll no longer dread doing it, and suddenly you will find you have time in your day for it (before, you might have made the excuse that you had no time). Suddenly, you will feel better about yourself and will be able to stick to a plan, all because you're doing something you enjoy. Your body will thank you.

Verse:

For your obedience is known to all, so that I rejoice over you, but I want you to be wise as to what is good and innocent as to what is evil. The God of peace will soon crush Satan under your feet. The grace of our Lord Jesus Christ be with you.
~ ROMANS 16:19–20

Prayer:

Lord, help me to be disciplined as I show up daily not to just look at the moment but the possibilities this life has to offer that you have gifted me. I pray that this life you have given me is a blessing to my spouse, or future spouse, my children, and my children's children, friends, and co-workers. I realize this will take effort on my part. Thank you for free will so that I can choose well today. Lord, I pray for the endurance to show up. Thank you for this temple you have gifted me. Help me to be a good steward of this body. If I am doing something that does not encourage the good health that I am striving to have, help me to get to the root of why am I doing it and replace it with truth in YOU, not a substitute. Amen.

Gauge to Grow:

1. After three minutes of Bible reading, write down something you read that stuck out to you and why.

2. How do you feel after a week of showing up for the three-minute rule or the thirty-minute rule? What will help you to incorporate this habit?

3. If struggling to be more consistent what would help you ensure you fulfill this commitment? Take the step today to incorporate success in this area.

Week 47

Difficulty in Direction

· ·

Start this week reflecting on
three wins from last week.

You are free to choose, but you are NOT free
to alter the consequences of your decisions.
~ Ezra Taft Benson

When moving forward, sometimes our own daily habits can get in the way. "Old habits die hard" is a familiar saying. Success is about making important habits easy, not difficult. What I mean by this is if you want to diminish TV time or video games, after each interaction, put the video game away up in the closet and remove it from sight. The more difficult it is to return to a bad habit, the less likely it is that you will reengage. We did this when we were having difficulty getting our kids when younger off video games. We unplugged it and put it away in the closet. When we realized it was taking too much of their time and they were not able to govern themselves to get off when we asked, we just removed the problem. We noticed a bad attitude after being on the game and being less willing to be helpful around the house. The right decision was to put it out of sight so that it was out of mind.

Think about an area you are trying to change. The more hoops you have to jump through to continue with the habit, the less likely you are to do so. What can you put in place that is in line with your desire to be your new self and will move you forward toward your other goals? You have to find a way to replace what inhibits your new habits of growth.

If you are taking classes online, it is easy to get carried away and check out, with your mind drawn away into its habitual escape routes (think: social media). Be mindful of what that habit might be and the times that it tears you away from your goal and best potential self. We are most comfortable with the automatic and the routine. But we should strive to cultivate habits offer lasting benefits, no matter how hard it might be to establish them in the beginning. Would a Facebook fast help? What benefits could fasting from social media give you?

Let us take it a step further; do not insert a comment here. Lol, hear me out. What would it look like to set yourself up when you leave a room so that when you return, the room is ready for you? Just process that thought for a second . . . when you leave the room or go to bed, and enter or wake up, is the room or space you occupy ready for you and or your family? What would this order bring? How can you inspire others in your household as you first eliminate clutter and welcome in a new level of tidiness? Is your car ready to go? What brings a smile to your face when you look at an empty clean sink, or a coffee pot ready to just push the button and out comes a glorious energy drink? Lol, or any space for that matter. When you enter it, do you find it is ready for you? How about an evening meal? Chop up your ingredients the night before and put it all in a crock pot so the next day you can just take it out of the fridge, turn it on, and arrive home after a long day to find dinner done, ready and waiting for you to enjoy. It's all about thinking three steps ahead, elevating your day and elevating your stress! Living in a stress-free zone is your home! What needs to be done for the efforts of lasting benefits?

Verse:

Therefore I tell you, do not be anxious about your life, what you will eat or what you will drink, nor about your body, what you will put on. Is not life more than food, and the body more than clothing? Look at the birds of the air: they neither sow nor reap nor gather into barns, and yet your heavenly Father feeds them. Are you not of more value than they? And which of you by being anxious can add a single hour to his span of life?

~ MATTHEW 6:25–27

Prayer:

Lord, I come to you desiring to be mindful of the joy I bring into the room, how I leave the room, and knowing you are there with me in the room. Help me to live in a way that glorifies you in every area I occupy. Help me to be aware of this area as I grow. Lord, help me to quiet my spirit before you and be fully engaged with the people and places you have placed me. Help me to be centered in the thoughts that are life-giving. Help me to bring about a positive outcome in all I do. Help me to live and model this in a way that is attractive to others. I need your consistency and peace, Lord. Help me to be present where you have placed me and a joy in my household. Amen.

Gauge to Grow:

1. Ask yourself, "Do I have the freedom to walk out of the room? Will I be able to return to the room with everything in its place and put it away? How can I find enjoyment as I go and return?" If you stay home, then think in terms of morning and evening.

2. Will the room be a positive environment to return to? What is the motion of the morning mood? Is more needed to be set in your living space? Are the dishes done before you leave the room? Is coffee set up for the next morning? Floor swept? A tidy home is a happy home. The overwhelming stress will be a thing of the past if you set up the household system to function in this way.

3. This also will cultivate positive overtones as you are preparing the space so that you will not be rushed and stressed in the space. Who you want to be is on the other side of your choices.

4. What did you unplug? Where did you put it when done, and how was your mood? Was being on a game or watching TV helpful? What areas were made possible when you put a time limit to it, unplugged it, or put it away when finished?

Week 48

Praise vs Confrontation

Start this week reflecting on
three wins from last week.

Praise in public; criticize in private.
~ VINCE LOMBARDI

This is important to process when dealing with loved ones, coworkers, and friends. When complimenting, do it in public if possible. Commend someone for a job well done, and don't wonder if they are looking for it. As human beings, we thrive on compliments and affirmation. When looking for the best in someone, you are sure to find it. When an area for criticism arises, do it privately and not when emotions are high. Think about the end result and ask your questions on the front end, which will help you achieve the positive outcome you desire. If the person is stressed, negative personality traits are more likely to be expressed. Keep in mind the power of the circle-back-around method. This involves processing, evaluating, and asking yourself where is the desired destination of the conversation. Ask questions that align with a positive outcome. Be mindful that the objective is not to make a point but to make a difference—a difference to that individual, a difference to that organization, a difference to that situation. No one will remember the point you made, but they will remember the difference and how you made them feel. We all want to be heard, so ask yourself, are you in it to share your side, or to learn, grow, and value others' points of view? Everyone wants someone in their corner. You can be that someone today. How important is being right to you? Do you find it difficult to not have the last word? There are so many ways to communicate in the English language. Think about how the person receives it, not how you come across it. Put yourself in their shoes, and if you don't know their shoes, ask their shoe size.

Verse:

Sow for yourselves righteousness; reap steadfast love; break up your fallow ground, for it is the time to seek the LORD, that he may come and rain righteousness upon you.

~ HOSEA 10:12

Prayer:

Lord, help me to love and care for the people you have placed in my life. I don't always need to agree but communicating care is always what is needed. Help me to see people with compassion and to have a desire to serve well. Lord, thank you for the people in my life. Thank you for in the hard times when I've needed people to support me and be in my corner. Help me to reach out and show compassion as I know I have gone through hard times and how much it is needed to show up for others even if I may not understand the whole picture yet. Thank you for being my Lord and savior in all that I go through. I thank you that I am not alone in it. Amen.

Gauge to Grow:

1. How can I serve others around me with a different point of view? Did they feel validated by me? If not, how can I work on that today?

2. Did someone come to mind who I have offended in the past and who I need to make right with today? If so, what is the best step I can take today in to make that right?

3. When emotions are high, how can I improve my listening from that heart and be less personally offended?

If I find myself being offended and in a bad mood after I spend time doing . . . what?

Reading Facebook comments? How can I set myself up to thrive and not get upset and take it personally?

Week 49

Run From or To

Start this week reflecting on
three wins from last week.

*We are what we repeatedly do. Excellence,
then, is not an act but a habit.*
~ ARISTOTLE

You are either running from something or running to something. Paul says in the Bible that we throw off the things that easily entangle us and run the race with endurance. When you're running from something, it's sprinting fast and furious.

Are you running from something or to something? Some of us need to decide to take off the backpack that is holding us back. For others of us, we need to start looking forward. Forward to the prize, forward to the calling, forward, embracing His plan and purpose for our life. Fix your eyes on Jesus Christ; fix your eyes on the author and perfecter, Jesus Christ. Regularly read the Bible, the living Word of Jesus Christ. The sixty-six books have the power to transform life. There are thirty-nine books in the Old Testament and twenty-seven books in the New Testament. What book of the Bible have you read that impacted your life? What verse is meaningful to you? When was the last time you read? Perhaps you are not interested in the Bible? Why? Did something take place that you are associating God with human hurt? Ask yourself why you have a reluctance to read the Bible. Get to the root of the hurt. Healing is on the other side of forgiveness.

Who are you helping? Who is alongside you sharing this race this journey together? You will hand each other a Gatorade bottle as you run the race of endurance. Endurance is effort, endurance is strategy, endurance is measuring your strengths and your personal abilities, and remaining focused on what's ahead. Who around you are helping your endurance? And who has been placed in your life to help you grow in your endurance? Or do you just want them to go away?

I had a lady tell me the struggle she was dealing with and asked for prayer. After we prayed, she thanked me for the meal that I made her while she was sick. She was quarantined in her room so that she would not contaminate her family with Covid. Guys, I don't even remember making the meal; I can't even tell you what the meal was. But I do know the care she experienced, and she shared with tears in her eyes that it meant so much to her. You see, in that moment we became more than friends. I put myself in her shoes and was moved to action wanting to meet her need and lighten her load. She felt cared for in her time of need for her and her family. The door was open for her to receive and desire to grow in her spiritual walk because of a meal I have no recollection of. Who are we helping today in our race?

Who are we caring for? Maybe it's a lost family member. Maybe it's a family member who has made some wrong choices and you feel like there's no hope for them. Maybe it's the next-door neighbor or a friend or someone that's sick who needs to know that they are seen. There is always hope. How can you be that hope that is needed today for someone?

What are we doing in this race to bring as many people as we can with us to run it? We all need each other. There are things that easily entangle us, and we must throw them off. Maybe it's fear, maybe it's stepping out of your comfort space to enter the race. Today could be the time to start. Maybe I'm being too independent. There is always a need, and God calls His people to fill it; whether or not we choose to do so is our choice. Take out that backpack of fear and inadequacy; stop qualifying yourself, because God doesn't call the qualified, he disqualifies the called. Read the following three names of people in the Bible that God qualified.

Moses—who claimed to not speak well
Gideon—led the army against their enemies with no prior experience
King David—called a man after God's own heart after he committed murder and adultery

That's just the three that comes to mind; the Bible is full of people who did not get it right the first time and yet did remarkable things for the Lord. You got this. We got this . . .

allow hope to fuel you today. Hope is the feeling of expectation and desire for something to take place.

Verse:

For we are God's handiwork, created in Christ Jesus to do good works, which God prepared in advance for us to do.
~ EPHESIANS 2:10

Not that we are competent in ourselves to claim anything for ourselves, but our competence comes from God.
~ 2 CORINTHIANS 4:5

Prayer:

Give me eyes to see, ears to hear, and the heart to understand what your Word wants to speak to me today. Lord, I want to leave this place better with an imprint of you marked by my life, not my mistakes. Thank you for your hope today. For people you have chosen with flaws and inadequacies made a lasting difference by yielding to your will and your ways. Help me to live with hope as I anticipate the next chapter in my life. I want to be truly alive. Thank you for my life with you, that I am chosen and called as your Word promises all who believe.

Gauge to Grow:

1. What are you feeling called to do?

2. What sets you apart? What is a dream in your heart you have yet to fully realize?

3. How do you want to be seen today? What attributes do you want to be known for?

4. In what way does your life speak and are you happy with what you say in actions?

Week 50

Marriage

Start this week reflecting on
three wins from last week.

A successful marriage requires falling in love many times,
always with the same person.
~ MIGNON MCLAUGHLIN

Marriage: two different people, two different perspectives, raised in two completely different households. How do they come together? How do they stay together, and how do they thrive in love? Do I have your attention? Marriage requires the ability to foster deep connections between two individuals, and I would add, over a lifetime of friendship and fostering truth and trust. How do we start well with the end in mind? Or do we? Planning for the wedding is for a day, planning for a lifetime is forever. How would our daily conversations look differently with the next season in mind? What does it look like? What can you start today that will help you in a healthy marriage? We all want it. How do we enjoy every day together knowing we are building up the next season of life together? For some, this may feel like a life sentence, so how do you change it to a life of thriving, love, and romance?

We plan so much for the wedding. How much did we plan for marriage? The way you show up every day and anticipate interaction with one another is crucial. A good marriage is a culmination of entering each other's space, ready to add to each other, serve the other, and show up ready to give and love. Easy to do on the honeymoon, but when life pulls and has demands, we get stressed, tired, and overwhelmed. Get back to the basics and remember to cultivate the marriage. Think about your words. How do you speak on the daily? Are you ready to see each other when you are home, and have you taken time to think well of each other? Speak well of each other? Checked in to see how the day was going? Some positive words to say to reinforce your marriage goals and strength-building bond: I'll be there for you, I love you, maybe you're right, I trust you, go for it, I got your back, how are you, I want you, I miss you, and you are amazing, what are you wearing?

The more details you can give after choosing one of these statements, the better it will resonate and cultivate a bond of trust, love, and friendship. Try it a few times then stay constant. It is a new behavior that needs to be managed. If you start with expectations of a quick result, you will not get long-lasting outcomes. Remember, consistency cultivates behavior in the direction of healthy, lasting benefits.

Keep in the forefront of your mind the goal. Take some time to write your marriage goals. We have as our goal not to just start out strong but to finish strong. What are some steps you can take this week to ensure you finish strong? We like to plan date nights, vacations, and personal dreams that we would like to reach someday. One of my dreams was to write this book. So many evenings and weekends I am writing, and we are not together like we usually are. However, this book is to help the women and children in India in the school and women education center that I helped to start over twenty-five years ago. So many people will be impacted with education, food, and health care by the proceeds of this book. This excites us both as we sacrifice to help reach our goals and celebrate together. Think of how this inspires you to do something together for someone else or an organization you can get involved in together. Start today with a forward motion of marriage. What impact are you making together as a couple? What do you stand for? What matters to you both? What unites you? What brings you closer? You are on the right track . . . keep going with ideas . . .

Verse:

However, let each one of you love his wife as himself,
and let the wife see that she respects her husband.
~ Ephesians 5:33

Prayer:

Lord, thank you for the opportunity to be a help mate. Not just a help mate but a good help mate. You've called us to lighten the load for our spouse. Remind us how important it is that we use our words to elevate and lift our spouse. And Lord, if you have not yet brought that person into our life, we pray for them now as you know who that person is, and we pray for your presence in their life and for our future. Lord, we trust your plan. We pray for plans, dreams, and God-sized goals we can look forward to together. We submit, so we can elevate our spouse. Help me to think and speak well of him and know the way he is wired also so that I can understand him better. Lord, thank you for your example to follow serving and loving our spouse. Lord, help us to look more like you as we care for our spouse and our marriage. We ask for your blessing and your favor over what you have joined together. And we claim right now a healthy marriage in our daily thoughts and actions. In Jesus' Name. Amen.

Gauge to Grow:

1. Practice saying three positive things you appreciate about the other daily. Remember, actions proceed with feelings. Just thinking it doesn't count; you have to say it. Look for ways to compliment, look for the positive, and acknowledge it. This grows your heart toward the other. I call this leaning into the relationship. That which you focus on will become larger.

2. Implement a 1, 1, 1 rule once a day. Connect for fifteen to thirty minutes. Set a timer at first to cultivate this healthy habit, which is also helpful if you have little ones needing your attention. This creates security in the family when

making children a priority as a married couple. Studies have shown that children experience night terrors and nightmares more often when they don't have the security of knowing mom and dad are good, healthy, and connected.

3. Go uninterrupted once a week on a date. This could be anything from taking a walk in the park to going on a drive to a lookout point or out to coffee or dinner. The point is to be intentional and make each other a priority. Planning is part of the enthusiasm—how you show up eager and with each other in mind. From what you wear to the topics of conversation, you are intentional in bringing up hopes, dreams, and aspirations.

4. And the final one is, once a year plan a trip and go together.

Week 51

Children Are to Be Reared

· ·

Start this week reflecting on
three wins from last week.

Children are like wet cement.
Whatever falls on them makes an impression.
~ HAIM GINOTT

How do you know if you are cultivating a healthy household? Let's be honest: we leave for work to get a break. Home care is hard care. Why? Because in it, our marriage and children are true indicators if all the relationships closest to us are healthy. It's an immediate reflection on us personally. Are we praying women? This relates to our awareness that we do not have all the answers and are in need of a mighty God who we need to turn to and humble ourselves before, praying and petitioning on behalf of our marriage and children.

I love moving and going at a fast pace, which goes with my ADHD tendencies. I have learned to harness my energy well to leverage my strengths. However, being busy does not equate to thriving; it means being busy doing. Let's keep in mind that we are human beings. It's when we slow down, walk slowly in a room, and pay attention to details so as to notice what's going on in the lives of our children. It matters. I make a game in my mind where, as I leave a room I make sure I discover three things I did not know before I entered the room. I make a point to care and be interested, which cultivates leaning in and loving well. How do you love your children well? What does loving your children well mean to you?

Three stark differences when entering a room . . . to give information is to share what you know. The second way is to enter with care. This will be apparent through curiosity, asking questions and looking for ways to help your child. Lastly, avoid the room altogether. To start with let me ask this question . . . Do you enjoy the people in your immediate family? What is the gauge of peace in the home? On a scale of 1–10 how would you rate the peace in your household? Are you pleased? Is this what you envisioned? What would you change? What would you add or take away? What do you cultivate when you enter and exit a room? What are you known for in your family? What do you want to be known for? What could you do to implement care for others when you arrive home and walk in? Are you that person? When others walk away from you, do they feel loved, cared for, and seen? What do your kids think is your strong attribute?

What would you say is their strong attribute? What are you known for in your home? Is it accurate? What are your children known for? How can you strengthen their character by walking it out yourself? Pause here and write out what comes to mind.

Verses:

Behold, children are a heritage from the Lord, the fruit of the womb a reward.

~ PSALM 127:3

So God created man in his own image, in the image of God he created him; male and female he created them. And God blessed them. And God said to them, "Be fruitful and multiply and fill the earth and subdue it, and have dominion over the fish of the sea and over the birds of the heavens and over every living thing that moves on the earth."

~ GENESIS 1:27–28

Prayer:

Lord, you are the God of the universe, the creator of all things in the earth, over the earth, and under the earth. We are created in your image. We thank you for the gift of life and the gift of children, family, and friends. Children are to be cared for, nurtured, and shown the way to the giver of life. Lord, you are the one we strive for them to know. To understand not just their last name but the name that is above all names. Jesus, we pray they know YOU as their personal Lord and savior. Help us to raise children as we direct them to you and your path. Lord, I know I'm not perfect and am flawed in many ways. I thank you that in my flaws and inadequacies, you have blessed me with children to pour into to call out for you and learn your ways. Please give me patience, love, and the ability to see each child uniquely and wonderfully made, with gifts, talents, and abilities to cultivate to the fullness of purpose to fulfill.

Gauge to Grow:

1. Do others want to be around our children, or do they just tolerate them? What can you do to encourage maturity in children you have or influence? A book I highly recommend is by the Ezzos: *What Every Kid Should Know Along the Way.*

2. Do you make excuses for their behavior? How can you apply accountability for behavior and decisions made? The Bible says, "Even a child is known by his doings whether they are wrong or right." Prov 20:11

3. Do you blame others and point the finger at missteps? Be mindful as to why. Ask yourself if it's a teachable moment and respond with, "We are working on that." And make it a point to truly work on it. Behavior starts at home. If not handled it extends. Take ownership, apply today, and do it again tomorrow.

Week 52

You Did It!

· ·

Wisdom is knowing the right path to take.
Integrity is taking it.
~ M. H. McKee

Congratulations!!!!! For making choices to grow and learn. The choice is all yours. You showed up daily devoted to right living and did the work. Examining yourself took a deep look within and made an effort to move forward this year.

As we examine our life over the past 52 weeks think about where you were and where you are now. Look at the seasons lived think about a name that would describe that season of life and ask yourself what did you learn? What was a big takeaway you are grateful for? How do you think you are doing now? How might that situation have helped you in becoming the person you are today? How did you give in? How did you stand up? How did you allow it to define you? How did you reframe the situation into a learning opportunity of growth over the past few months? Are you desiring to continue to put the time and effort into becoming a person of character and integrity? It's not quick; it takes time to be intentional and requires daily sacrifice. Character is defined by how your habits, motives, and thoughts relate to morality, particularly as it concerns integrity. Character is defined as "your moral self," the "crown of a moral life," and is referred to as a "moral structure," something you build through various trials. Keep going keep growing, you have come so far. I am so proud for you and so grateful for the time being devoted to growth and not settling for mediocre living.

Verse:

Be strong and courageous. Do not be afraid; do not be discouraged, for the Lord your God will be with you wherever you go.

~ JOSHUA 1:9

Prayer:

Lord, thank you for the growth I am experiencing right now. Thank you that I am not who I once was and I am going toward my future best self. Help me to enjoy the process and see the best outcome out of each experience. When I'm upset, help me to regulate myself so the enemy cannot steal what has already been done in helping me experience the freedom found only in you. Thank you for the forgiveness I have received and help me in turn to forgive others. In Jesus' Name, I pray. Amen.

Chances are you did not reach where you are overnight. It took a series of decisions along the way. What can you implement today that will set you on a different course and direction? What would a wise decision walking out in your life look like?

Ask yourself, are you teachable? Often, we have a finger-pointing problem, Adam and Eve style. You see, from the beginning, blaming each other and lying was the default. Pointing and finding flaws takes no effort. Stepping out and doing things outside of God's best for our lives will take us down a road we have no business going down.

Taking responsibility and owning our actions in an honest, transparent way reaches the heart, causes change, and sets you on a different course of life. Read in Genesis about the garden. Where did they go wrong? How can you relate?

Verse

Better the poor whose walk is blameless than a fool whose lips are perverse.

~ PROVERBS 19:1

The righteous lead blameless lives: blessed are their children after them.

~ PROVERBS 20:7

Prayer:

Lord, thank you for this amazing journey I am on. I am growing and changing so much and am so glad I am choosing to put one foot in front of the other to walk out the next that you have in store for my life. I thank you that I don't have all the answers. I thank you for help and discernment from your word and people that I know care about me wanting the best for me. Help me to have a receiving spirit approachable and receptive. Help me to ask the right questions as I'm longing to do the right things daily. I am blessed, I am loved, I am unique! Thank you for making me! Amen

Ask yourself the following questions . . .

1. What made me proud this year?

2. What did I learn this year?

3. Who did I lead this year?

4. What held me back this year?

5. Do I still love what I do?

6. Am I willing to pay the price, again, this year?

7. What's the most important thing right now?

8. What do I need to change?

9. What is my word for the year?
John Maxwell

Gauge to Grow:

1. What did I learn most about myself as I journeyed through this book?

2. What chapter did I enjoy the most?

3. What was a rub I experienced and how did I overcome it? What does that say about me?

. . . .

Learning to Lean in Deeper

. . . .

I n quiet spirit, no static noise is allowed in. That's when I can breathe, expanding my lungs to breath life and leading me to a life that is higher than I.

What can happen if we learn to quiet our minds and lean in? Allowing space to learn, grow, and thrive means less talking, looking at the area you most want to grow in, and taking one forward action step daily. This can shift a negative to a positive, purposeful time investment.

Think about what thoughts you had at the beginning of this book. Consider areas in which you found yourself stuck or going in circles. What was your biggest breakthrough? Look at how much you have grown spiritually, mentally, emotionally, and physically. What was the moment you realized you wanted to grow? What area have you avoided growing in? Why are you hesitant? What did it take to step in the right direction? What was your biggest hesitation? What emotion do you feel was primarily holding you back? What questions did you have that are now answered?

What are you doing daily that is the most important area for you that you have improved in? What did you change or shift? On a scale of 1–10 how are you doing in the process of becoming the best version of yourself? What could you add to make that number a 10?

What are you waiting for that has been spoken to you more than once that you dismiss? How did you show up more enthusiastically for something you were on the fence about? Is what you are thinking and saying improved over the past 52 weeks of reading this book?

We tend to shut down or lash out when hurt or do not feel heard. When you want to go forward into the next and you feel the push back know the blessing is on the other side of it. What is the area you want the walls of your heart to come down?

Verse

May these words of my mouth and the meditation of my heart be pleasing in your sight, lord, my rock and my redeemer.

~ PSALM 19:14

Prayer:

Lord, I thank you for being here with me right now in this room, in this space guiding me and comforting me right now. I thank you that I am not alone in what I am going through and you know everything I need right now in this moment. You are my rock you are my redeemer. Thank you for this season of growth and development. I ask you to help me silence the noise that takes from my peace and my sense of belonging. As I speak to you Lord, I ask for clarity as I silence the static and turn up the calm only you can give. I thank you for all you have done in my life and I praise your name for you alone are good!

Pick three of the above questions that apply to you and be intentional this week. As we grow, the phrase "hurts so good" comes to mind. When you are going, you are growing. Going forward in the application is key. Showing up to pray, read, apply, rinse, and repeat. Pray so you have strength more than you own on your own; read to refocus and gain a new perspective. Make application of your new insights in your daily routine and you will reach growth as a result. Evaluate how much you have grown. Then show up the next day and do it again.

Trust the process. Taking steps daily to maximize time is essential for desired results.

Tell yourself, "Just do it" three times as soon as you wake up. This will help rewire your brain as self-talk is vital when starting a new pattern. You got this. Health is important, you are important. Your life is important. Do what you were made to do, go where you are meant to go and show up with the best version of yourself today. Today is the day you start and finish strong. Today's a new day, make it count for your best self tomorrow.

About the Author

Growing up in Oregon has given me a deep connection to nature, and spending time outdoors invigorates me. Whether I'm hiking in the stunning Columbia River Gorge or sharing meaningful hunting trips with my father in Livingston, Montana, these experiences refresh my spirit.

It reminds me that life's simplest moments hold the greatest significance. I moved to New York 25 years ago, married my wonderful husband, and now have three adult kids, Michael 21, Shauna 20 and Matthew, soon to be 18. What a ride it has been.

After dedicating years to teaching elementary students, I'm now devoted to inspiring growth as a full-time pastor and Life Coach at Next Step Victory LLC, guiding individuals toward a brighter future.

Thank you from the depths of my heart for taking this incredible leap towards personal growth! Your investment not only transforms your life but also brightens the futures of countless children in India at Grace School, where love, care, and exceptional education thrive.

As a co-founder of Grace School, established in 1998, the proceeds of this book will help further advance our thriving multiple schools.